WHY I DIDN'T

THE SHELDON KENNEDY STORY

SAY ANYTHING

WHY I DIDN'T

THE SHELDON KENNEDY STORY

SAY ANYTHING

SHELDON KENNEDY
WITH JAMES GRAINGER

INSOMNIAC PRESS

Library and Archives Canada Cataloguing in Publication

Kennedy, Sheldon
    Why I didn't say anything : the Sheldon Kennedy story / Sheldon Kennedy ; with James Grainger.

Includes index.
ISBN 1-897178-07-7

1. Kennedy, Sheldon. 2. Sexually abused teenagers--Canada.
3. Sexual abuse victims--Canada--Biography. 4. Hockey players--Canada--
Biography. I. Grainger, James, 1967- II. Title.

GV848.5.K45A3 2006   796.962'092   C2005-907620-8

The publisher gratefully acknowledges the support of the Canada Council, the Ontario Arts Council and the Department of Canadian Heritage through the Book Publishing Industry Development Program.

Printed and bound in Canada

Insomniac Press
192 Spadina Avenue, Suite 403
Toronto, Ontario, Canada, M5T 2C2
www.insomniacpress.com

 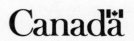

DEDICATION

This book is dedicated to my daughter, Ryan. Thank you for giving me a reason to start looking and dealing with the abuse and addictions I suffered from. I love you and am so proud of you for just being YOU. You are my sunshine everyday, Ryan, and for that I am grateful.

I would also like to dedicate this book to the people who still suffer from abuse/addiction. I pray that you find the courage to dig deep to the pain and start to recover. I am writing this book to give people hope that there is a way out, and that we can be free inside. I never ever believed that that could come true. Only when I was left with the choice to die or surrender was I able to start working to find the way out. Rigorous Honesty, Trust, Faith all followed with action was the way I found to work. The twelve steps of AA worked for both the abuse and addiction, I am so grateful for the opportunity to have found these steps. It is about living, something that was distorted for me my whole life.

Today I am a very grateful man. The big thing for me is always to remain teachable, and remember progress, not perfection.

"God grant me the serenity to accept the things I cannot change, courage to change the things I can, and the wisdom to know the difference." This prayer sums it up for me; Keeping It Simple is the key to my freedom. My goal was to simplify the confusion surrounding abuse/addiction. I feel that we are confused enough already in our heads. I wanted to get to the point and lay it out in a simple but honest way that we could all relate to. I hope this book gives you the courage to change.

ACKNOWLEDGEMENTS

I have had a lot of people help me along the way and would like to thank a few that never wavered through all of my craziness.

Wayne McNeil—Thank you for always believing in me. You put our friendship on the line when you wrote the letter explaining how bad my lifestyle really was, and for that I am grateful. You are a great friend and have always been there through the ugly, fun, desperate, and now grateful times. You are a great friend. Thanks, Wayner.

Dayna, Lindsay, Braden, and Marianna McNeil—Dayna, thanks for all your kindness and dedication to the issues of abuse. You are a great lady and a good friend. Most importantly, you are a great mother, and have raised three of the most genuine kids I know. Lindsay, Braydon, Marianna, thank you for loving me for who I was, not what I was. Your friendship is more than you'll ever know.

Dr. Brian Shaw—Your message was always consistent: "I am always there for you Shelly," and yes indeed you were. You have helped me and many others receive the help they need. One thing I learned was that I needed to do the work. Someone else wasn't going to get me sober. Brian, I am very grateful for all you have done for me. You are a good friend. Thanks, man.

NHL/NHLPA substance abuse program: Dr. Lewis, Dan Cronin, Dr. Shaw—Thank you for never giving up. I am sure I tested your patience more than once. I hope at some point I can give back. Thanks for all you have done. Ryan and I are so grateful.

Ali Dickson Gray—Ali, thank you for having the courage to come and rescue me from the darkness. You saw me at my darkest point and I know it wasn't pretty, so thank you for having the courage to still be my friend.

Lionel and Joannie Conacher—Thanks for supporting me. I respect the two of you a lot. What impresses me is the way you raise your kids. They're great. I consider you and your family very good friends and hope it can only grow. Maybe I will teach you how to barefoot, big boy.

Jeff Jackson—You've always been there, man, I can't believe I didn't scare you off. Thanks for being strong, my friend.

Catherine Loubier—Thanks for all you have done. You helped me get to a point in recovery I have never been before and for that I am grateful.

Lanny McDonald — Thank you for all your support. Without your help so much would not have been possible.

Paul, Jana, Ryan, Niah, and Wilson Hickie—Paul, thanks for being a good stepdad to Ryan, thank you. Jana, well you were the reason that I first decided to look at the abuse. I will never be able to explain how important you were and are in my life. Thank you for all your love and thank you for never giving up on me. I am so grateful that you are happy, Jana. I will always respect you for what you have done for me. Thanks.

AARC (Alberta Adolescent Recovery Centre)—I love this place and everybody involved. Thank you all for my sobriety and I wish you all another 24. Now let's go help some kids.

Brian Evans—Thanks for everything, living the way I did, good legal counsel was always a good thing. Thanks Brian.

Bob Probert—Probie, I love you, man, you helped me a lot as I stumbled through life. I am grateful for the opportunity to have played and lived with you, and I am proud to call you a friend. You are a good man, Bob, I know that. You are a gentle man with a big heart when you're sober. I hope you believe you deserve to have freedom from the mind. I love you and your family.

Thank you all who supported the Sheldon Kennedy Foundation. There is a lot more to do so keep on trucking.

God bless all of you and your families. No, I am not religious, I am spiritual. Now that is pretty wild, eh?

And my family, Mom, Troy and Sherri, thanks for always sticking up for me even when it was tough to do so. I am very grateful to have a family that sticks up for one another and also confronts when one needs to be confronted. Thanks and I love you all.

Chapter One

I was born in 1969 in Brandon, a small city in southwestern Manitoba, but my parents soon moved my older brother, Troy, and I up to Thompson, a town about 500 miles north of Winnipeg. The winters there are long and cold. Like most towns on the Prairies, just about everyone, young and old, participates in some form of winter sports. Most kids are strapping on a pair of skates shortly after they learn to walk, and Troy and I were no exception.

In fact, most of my earliest memories seem to occur on a long, white ice surface. My parents brought me to one of the outdoor rinks in Thompson when I was two years old, and after strapping on my brother's old skates, I went out onto the ice. According to my mother, I stood tall on my skates and did not bend at the ankles. I must have learned to keep my ankles straight from watching Troy and my parents on the ice.

The next year, my mother registered me and Troy for figure skating lessons in Thompson. Mom would spend half the morning bundling me and

Troy and our new baby sister, Sherri, and then walking over to the arena pulling Sherri in our little sleigh. The figure skating lesson was supposed to go from 1:30 p.m. to 2:30 p.m. but it usually wrapped up by 2:00. Mom realized that the ice was booked until 2:30 and asked the teacher if Troy and I could stay on the ice and just skate around. The teacher didn't have a problem with us staying behind, so a whole half hour every week, Troy and I got the whole rink to ourselves. Those were great times. There was no pressure to perform or learn a new technique. We would skate around and fall on our butts and get up again. That year at the ice show, I got to skate out onto the ice and present our teacher with a bouquet of flowers. It was my first experience performing on the ice in front of a large crowd and I executed the skate well, especially considering that I was only three years old.

The following winter, we were living in Winnipeg. Dad made us a little rink in the backyard to practice skating and handling the puck. One day, my dad brought home a puck that was twice the size and weight of a normal puck and told us that he would play in net as long as we used that big puck. We didn't like the puck but it was great to have a goalie and to be out on the ice with our dad. We didn't realize at the time that by using a heavier puck, Dad was forcing us to develop co-ordination and muscle strength in our hands and arms. By the end of the winter, Troy and I could raise the puck a foot or so off the ice with a well-practiced wrist shot. When we began to use a normal puck again, it seemed to fly from the blades of our sticks.

Troy was ready to start playing ice hockey in the local house league. My dad bought equipment for me and Troy. Every Saturday Troy got into his equipment to play at the outdoor rink where the league held its games. Luckily there was another ice surface next to Troy's game, so Dad let me get into my equipment and play with another kid on the empty ice while Troy played. My parents could see how much I loved hockey and wanted to make sure that I didn't feel left out.

The next year, I was finally old enough to play house league. Troy and I played at indoor and outdoor rinks. The rest of the year, we played soccer, lacrosse, baseball, and road hockey. Our parents didn't have to push to get us into sports—we weren't interested in doing much else!

When I was six, my parents bought a farm just outside Elkhorn, Manitoba, a little town a couple hours north of the American border and about three hours west of Winnipeg. In other words, we lived in the middle of nowhere. When people ask me how isolated we were, I just tell them that the kids at school used to bring McDonald's wrappers in for show and tell. That was a taste of the big city for us farm kids.

Elkhorn was a typical Prairie town. The climate was harsh, the work days were long. Life revolved around the farms, the church, the co-op, the bars and donut shops, and the local Legion. But the real centre of the community were the hockey and curling rinks. You live your life outdoors in those Prairie towns, so you might as well learn to enjoy yourself, even in the long cold winters.

My family had a 600-acre dairy farm and about 160 head of cattle. You had to milk the cows at 5:30 a.m. and again in the afternoon every day, whether you felt like it or not. The cows have to be fed and they need a hell of a lot of fresh hay. It's hard, slow work and if you don't get it done, no one else will. My parents were constantly worried about money and the weather and the cows. There always seemed to be a drought in Manitoba, and how were we going to feed 160 cows? It was not uncommon to work 22- and 23-hour workdays. You got up, worked, played a bit of hockey, and went to bed. Most days there hardly seemed time to sit down and catch your breath.

Troy, Sherri, and I were expected to help out around the farm before and after school. There was always work that needed to be done. There was hardly time to sit down and eat. My brother helped my mom milk the cows every morning and after school. My sister prepared the meals. And I helped my father out in the fields and in the barns. I was treated like a man by the age of ten. I took the blame for what went wrong. It was pretty rough at times, and I often felt more like my dad's hired man than his son.

He was a very angry man around the farm. I've never quite figured out why he was so angry; maybe it was because the hard life of a farmer wore down his nerves. All I know is that he took a lot of that anger out on me. Maybe it was because he and I spent so much time together working in the fields and the barns but I always seemed to be getting on his bad side and earning myself a smack or a full-on beating. Nothing I did was ever good enough. I couldn't confront him directly, but like any kid, I found ways of acting out my pain and frustration. I was always the funny kid, a little hyper, and one of the ways I acted out was to be the joker. I liked to play the clown and make people laugh but this just seemed to make my dad even more angry. I began to shut down emotionally a lot of the time when I was at home, and this made it hard for me to get close to my brother, sister, and mother, even though they tried to be good to me. They also found it hard to get close to me.

I carried around a lot of that anxiety around with me outside of the home. I was so anxious that I found it hard to pay attention in school. I was convinced, like quite a few of my teachers, that I was too stupid to get good grades. Why bother trying? My marks were never very good, which made Dad even more angry at me. There were many scenes around the dinner table when Dad would ask me and my brother and sister about school. I almost never had any good news to pass on. Dad would lose his temper when he heard about my latest test scores and he would call me an idiot. I would vow to bring my marks up. But the angrier he got about my marks, the more worried I got about my school work, and the more I worried about my school work, the harder I found it to pay attention when I was at school. My marks got even worse, and the cycle continued.

I wasn't the only one who was nervous in the presence of my dad. The whole family walked on eggshells while he was around. We worried about his moods constantly. We were scared to make a mistake, scared to say anything that might set him off. It was better to be quiet when he was around, so we were most of the time. It was a little like living on the side of a mountain and worrying that if you were too loud or said the wrong thing, you would bring an avalanche down on the house. But there were plenty of good times when company came over. Dad liked to play the role of the boisterous fun-loving guy around other people, pretending that everything was great on the farm and in the family. When people came to visit, we pretended that we were living the Canadian dream: a happy family safe behind their picket fence.

Life was also good a lot of the time. When you live out in the country, you get to spend a lot of time outdoors. Dad loved to go snowmobiling and waterskiing in the summer. He also loved to go to tractor pulls, which are always big events in farming communities. My parents were worried and overworked but they made time to help us out with hockey and figure skating. We skated and played hockey on a pond out in the back in the winter and the rest of the time, we played road hockey. If it was too cold or dark outside, my brother and I played living-room hockey, doing a lot of damage to Mom's piano in the process. All the boys loved playing hockey. We often played two or three games of ice hockey a day, plus road hockey in between games if there was time.

There's no substitute for playing hockey and skating night and day. You get to the point where skating becomes as natural as going for a walk and the stick becomes an extension of your hands. My sister was getting involved in figure skating, and after watching her, I began performing axles in my hockey skates or jumping in the air and dancing on the ice. I also used to show my parents how well I could skate even with my laces untied.

In time, Troy and I became excellent hockey players. Sherri was a great figure skater. The Kennedy family was admired in the farming community. We were driven and we seemed to succeed at whatever we tried. My father helped coach the hockey team. My dad was very different at the games than when he was at home. He was an assistant coach, so he didn't make a lot of calls on the ice. He opened the door during line changes and gave the players little bits of advice on their game between shifts. He took my brother and I and the other players wherever we needed to go, and I've always been grateful that he gave us that support. My friends all loved my dad and looked up to him. He always pushed us to excel at the game but he wasn't like a lot of hockey fathers, whose only goal in life seemed to be to make their sons into NHL stars. He was paying for our hockey and helping coach the team and driving us to other towns to play, so he expected us to do our best and take the game seriously, but he never tried to force us to become professional athletes.

Since my parents worked so much, my father needed to have my brother and I playing on the same team, even though I was at least a year younger than the guys I played with. This ultimately made me a better hockey player. I had to keep up with players who were older, faster, and stronger than me. I wouldn't have had to work as hard as I did if I'd stayed back with players my own age. I was always playing an age group ahead so that I could travel with my brother, but I was a good enough player to get away with playing with older boys. If I was supposed to play in bantam hockey, I would be playing in midget, and so forth, throughout my childhood and into my early teens.

We had a team of about fifteen players, and out of that team, about nine or ten of us played junior and about four or five of us played semi-pro. I was the only one who made it to the NHL, but when we were younger, we each thought we'd be playing on our favourite team. From a very early age, I can remember dreaming about playing in the NHL, skating down the giant ice surface in front of all those fans and cameras and scoring an overtime goal.

Our team played up to 100 games a year, and since Elkhorn only had one team per tier, we did a lot of travelling to other towns. Tournaments would be organized so that teams from all over the region could play. We had a great group of kids. It was a blast. I was playing hockey, travelling on the bus with my Bobby Orr lunch box. I had a passion for the game and never felt better than when I was out on the ice on my skates.

We had one of the best teams in a province that had some very good teams with some very good players. Theoren Fleury, Mike Keane, John Ferguson, Jr.—all these guys were playing on rival teams. But we were too good for most of the other teams in our age group. It was ridiculous—we were winning games 35 to nothing. There were games where my brother and I hardly left the ice because we barely had enough players to make a team but we still won almost every time we played. There was one year that I don't remember us losing a single game. We were eventually asked to leave the league, so we just practiced and played in tournaments. We were driving to Winnipeg for tournaments and sometimes even beating the best teams, including the Winnipeg Monarchs and Brandon Wheat Kings, who were in the Triple A Midget league.

People in the stands would call us country hicks. You could tell we were from the sticks. The other teams all had new equipment and matching jerseys. But each of our players had a slightly different jersey. On the front of one shirt would be the name of a local livestock company that had just enough money to sponsor one jersey, and on another would be the name of a creamery or a construction company. So the players each had a different logo on their jersey but we'd still go in there and kick ass.

I was never the best player on that team (my brother and Teddy Taylor's son, who went on to play for the Huston Aeros, were the top players) but I was the youngest, so people noticed me. I didn't have a lot of pressure on me, but I was still playing on the second or third line and having a great time. I looked up to the older players on the team. I got along great with the older kids who I played hockey with and I began hanging around with older people as a result. I can't remember ever hanging around with kids my own age, though that never made me feel lonely or depressed. That was just the way it was.

The kids who I went to school with were a little jealous of my hockey success. A lot of them also didn't like the fact that I hung around with the older boys most of the time. The older boys thought I was as funny as hell—one of those tough little scrappers who was always trying to wind everybody up. They used to egg me on to tease kids my own age, and I was glad to go along.

Their families were often jealous too. As anyone who has grown up in a small town knows, your community and the stores and houses and public places are as familiar to you as your own living room. I knew just about everybody's name and family—who they were friends with and who they were on the outs with that week. You walk around recognizing every face and knowing what you need to know about them. Everyone knows everyone in a little town like Elkhorn. They know your family. They know your history. And they know how many goals you scored—or didn't score—in the last hockey game. So being successful on a great hockey team where everyone was older than me did not make me popular with a lot of the parents of kids my age. They were never outright hostile but they often wouldn't associate with me. Silence was their most powerful weapon. And the teams below us were not doing well at the time, which made matters even worse. Our team, in many ways, did not associate with the rest of the town. In some ways we were above and apart from everything in the town, but we were all having such a great time that I rarely ever noticed. And in spite of some of the hostility, the town was proud of our success. People all over the Prairies were starting to know about the tiny town of Elkhorn.

Until about the age of ten or so, you're just out there having fun on the ice and fantasizing about playing in the NHL, but once you get to a certain age, you start to wonder if you really could play in the big leagues, and if so, how would you go about getting there. All of these thoughts were going through my mind, and as time went by, it seemed like maybe the dream could come true. My name was suddenly being mentioned with other kids' names when people talked about the WHL draft. It all started to seem possible.

I can remember the excitement when I first began to be noticed by junior teams that were scouting for younger players. I was twelve years old and junior teams were already trying to make plans to get me and Troy on their rosters. I started dreaming more and more about making it to the NHL, but I knew that the only way that was going to happen was to impress the scouts who were increasingly showing up in the stands.

I wasn't the only player being scouted. Our team was turning heads wherever we went, so scouts representing the minor league teams would make a point of catching our games. As a hockey player, you are told from a very young age that if you want to get anywhere and advance in the game, you have to impress the scouts. You've heard about these powerful men since you laced up your skates in your first house-league game. They decided who got invited to the tryout camps. They were the ones who began to mention your name to the coaches who could draft or trade for you one day, and those coaches and managers would have even more power over you if you did make it into the minor leagues. They could put you on the first line or sit you on the bench. If they didn't like your attitude, they could trade you to a bad team or send you home to your family, and then you'd never have another chance.

But to even get to the minors, you had to catch the eye of a scout. In a system where word of mouth and reputation decides the fate of a young player, the opinion of a scout can either make or break your career. These men, and the coaches and managers they report to, are like gods in the eyes of the young players. You know where they are sitting in the stands and you know who's going to be reading their scouting reports the next day.

The scouts were keeping an eye on almost every player on our team, so we were all excited for each other. There were a few guys on the team who we figured weren't going to make it, but everyone else had a good shot at making the juniors. Even the guys who probably weren't going to make it into the juniors were given a shot at a junior camp.

We were usually in and out of a town just long enough to get ready for the game, play, get showered and changed and then head back home. There was always a guy on the team who could pass for eighteen and he would buy a case of beer but there really wasn't enough time in the winter to do much drinking. You were either working or playing hockey or doing school work, and since we all lived on farms, we lived pretty far from each other. In the summers, after you'd done your chores, you would ride your bike and go out and drink with your friends somewhere. In those small farm towns you learn to drink early and often. Alcohol is often the social lubricant of small-town life. Most people learn to keep their drinking under control but almost everyone enjoys a drink with their friends. It's part of the culture. But for me the real problem with alcohol came later, after coach Graham James entered my life.

Chapter Two

Every summer, my parents managed to scrape together enough money to send me and Troy to hockey camp for a couple of weeks. It was an opportunity for us to sharpen our skills with a variety of professional coaches and the occasional ex-NHL player. My father also knew that the coaches at the camp often had connections with the scouts and management of the minor-league hockey teams all us kids hoped to play for. Being spotted at hockey camp was one of the best ways to catch the eye of the men who decided who would climb to the next hockey tier. From there, anything seemed possible if you tried hard enough.

Hockey camp was also a great way for us to get away from the tensions and constant arguments of life back on the farm. My parents' marriage seemed to be getting worse as we kids got older. Mom and Dad barely spoke to each other at times, unless my Dad was complaining about something, usually me and my latest screw up.

Troy and I had been earning quite a name for the Kennedy clan the previous season. Our junior rights had already been traded by the Brandon Wheat Kings, but we were eager to improve our games and make a good impression with the coaches at the camp. We were both pumped and full of expectation when my father dropped us off at the Andy Murray Hockey School in Winnipeg in the summer of 1982. As he said goodbye, Dad reminded us to listen to the coaches and treat them with respect. No fooling around! The coach is so respected. Your parents send you away and tell you, "Do whatever he says." At that age, you listen, especially when you've had an upbringing like mine where you never talked back to the person in charge. You listen to the coach because he is in charge and because he is your first step to playing pro.

Shortly after checking in, I met Graham James, the man who would change my life forever. Graham was an ex-school teacher who had risen rapidly through the ranks of minor-league hockey coaching after the leaving the game at eighteen because of chronic asthma. He was known as a hotheaded and eccentric coach who understood the game and knew how to motivate his players and improve their offensive and defensive skills. He could quote Shakespeare and curse the players and refs with the best of them. He also had a reputation for involving himself in his players' lives off the ice, taking a personal interest in their welfare, especially where school was concerned. "No matter how good a player you are, it will never be enough to get you through life," Graham was known to tell his players; "You need to do well in school and give something back to your community."

I certainly wasn't overly impressed when I saw Graham for the first time. He was a little on the chubby side and seemed a little nervous and not quite comfortable in his own skin. But once he was on the ice and interacting with the players, he exuded confidence. It was obvious that he knew the game of hockey and loved watching it played well. He had a funny and interesting way of saying things that you'd heard a thousand times before so that you thought about them in a new way. He was very popular with the players and the other staff at the camp.

Graham recognized my talent right away. He gave me tips on how to improve my game and made a point of singling me out in the drills and practices. Off the ice, he bought me pop and chips and other snacks. I was totally flattered that this smart worldly man was taking an interest in me. I'd never met anyone who seemed to know so much about hockey and the world outside of the little town where I'd grown up.

Over the two weeks, I found out that besides having coached the Winnipeg South Blues and Fort

Garry Blues to provincial titles, he was now working as a scout for a number of junior teams. This
made him even more of a hero in my eyes. Men
like Graham were put on a pedestal. They held the
keys to the kingdom we were all dreaming about:
the NHL. If a man in Graham's position liked you
and admired the way you handled yourself on the
ice, they saw to it that you made the right connections and moved up the minor league ladder. Piss
off someone like Graham or get on their bad side,
and you might as well stay home.

Shortly after that camp, Graham began courting my parents. He would phone up and tell them
what great careers Troy and I had ahead of us and
how he hoped to coach us in the future. His star
was still rising in the coaching ranks and he was
now the coach of the Winnipeg Warriors, a WHL
team. He began trying to acquire my and Troy's
junior rights, which were held by the Brandon
Wheat Kings, another WHL team. Eventually,
Graham traded Randy Cameron, one of his
Warriors players, for our rights, and then phoned
me and asked if I would like to play for the
Warriors. I couldn't believe it. One of the best
coaches in the West was asking me, a fourteen-
year-old kid, if I wanted to play in the WHL. It
seemed like the chance of a lifetime.

In April of 1984, Graham invited me down to

Winnipeg for a week to watch the Lions Tournament, the biggest minor league tournament in Manitoba. He also arranged for me to play in a few of the games. He told my parents that I could stay with him in his Winnipeg apartment. Mom and Dad couldn't put me on the bus fast enough.

Graham met me at the station and took me straight to the arena. While we were watching the tournament, he asked me questions about my life that nobody had ever asked me. He asked me how I got along with my dad, how I liked playing on my team, how I felt about school. I opened up to him immediately, especially when he asked me about my relationship with my dad. I wasn't used to being asked about my feelings and opinions about things, and I sure wasn't used to being listened to with so much interest and attention. I told Graham that my dad was never happy with anything I did, and he seemed to really listen to what I was saying. He seemed to care.

We went out to dinner that night and then went back to his apartment. I was a little startled when we first walked in. The walls were covered in photographs and newspaper clippings of the players he'd coached over the years. I recognized some of them who had gone on to play in the NHL. After listening to him talk about hockey all day and seeing the way he was treated by the men and players

Playing for the Winnipeg South Blues, the second of Graham's teams that I played for.

around the rink, I knew he was an important man. The pictures on the wall just drove that point home more. I was thrilled to be with him. I didn't want to screw things up, and because he'd been so open and caring with me, I wanted him to like and respect me.

I also noticed, as I was getting ready for bed, that the windows of his apartment were blacked out with cardboard, as if he didn't want any light to get in. I was too nervous to ask about this. Maybe he liked to sleep in in the mornings, or maybe there were a lot of lights outside the building that I hadn't noticed on the way in.

He set up a cot for me beside his own bed, which also seemed a little odd to me at the time, but I didn't say anything. He put the lights out. With the windows taped and covered with cardboard, the apartment was pitch black. I was nervous but also very tired. It had been an exciting day on so many levels. Scenes from the day kept replaying in my mind. I could see the older players skating across the ice and remember Graham's expert comments on their play.

I was almost asleep when I heard Graham crawling around near the end of the cot. He started rubbing my feet, telling me that a foot rub was the best thing for the body after a hard day. I felt very uncomfortable but let him do it for awhile.

Eventually, I couldn't take it anymore and pushed him away and put my feet under the blankets. I heard him crawl away back to his bed. I thought that that would be the end of it.

It was just the beginning. I heard Graham moving around in the dark on the other side of the room. Then I heard him looking for something. A few seconds later, he opened a closet door and seemed to pick up a heavy object. There was more movement as he made his way back to his bed, and then he flicked on the lights. When I opened my eyes in the sudden brightness, I saw Graham sitting in bed cradling a shotgun. He was smiling, but it wasn't a smile I'd ever seen before. For a couple of seconds, I barely recognized the man sitting on the bed. He looked crazed. His eyes were almost glowing in his head. He was out of his head, but I'd never seem him looking so sure of himself and what he was doing. He looked like a man in total control of the situation. As he sat in bed cradling the shotgun, he began talking about how he loved to hunt ducks, how he loved going out and getting them in his sights and shooting them. Then he began moving and jumping around the room with the gun, acting as if he'd like nothing better than to kill something.

He didn't have to say anymore. He knew the effect the gun would have on me. I was alone in a strange place with a strange man who held the keys to the world that I had wanted to be part of since I was a little kid. He was a man who I'd been told to look up to and obey. He knew all of this, and he knew that he could use his authority and my fear and ignorance to get me to do something that I didn't understand and didn't want to be a part of. He had been fondling my feet in the dark, coming on to me, knowing how frightened I would be. When I resisted, he went away to get his next weapon, and when he turned on the light, he showed me what would happen if I didn't co-operate.

After showing me the gun for a while, he turned out the lights again, and this time, when he came to my bed, I didn't resist. He started to rub my feet again. I did what so many sexual assault victims have done before: I pretended to be asleep. I was like someone trapped in a bad dream who thinks that if they just lie still enough, the big monster in the room will pass them by and leave them alone. Of course, this strategy never works but it allows the victim to create the illusion that what is happening to them is not real. Then Graham pulled my underwear off and tried to perform oral sex on me but I pulled away. He didn't try that again that night. Instead, he touched me all over until he'd satisfied himself, then he finally went to bed.

The next morning, he acted as if everything was

normal between us, that this kind of thing happened all the time and wasn't really worth talking about. He was even joking around with me like we were old buddies. I was numb the whole day, in a state of shock, but amazingly I could still talk and eat and also act as if nothing had happened. We went to the arena again and watched hockey all day and talked about our lives some more. He analyzed the game and pointed out what certain players were doing right and wrong, and he asked my opinion on what was happening on the ice. Even with the fear and numbness and shock, I still felt flattered that he asked my opinions about hockey and let me in on the secrets of the game.

The abuse happened for the next four nights. Graham forced me to take steam baths and showers with him, and at night, he visited me in my cot and masturbated on me. After the first night, I went into a kind of protective shell, like an accident victim using all of their energy to protect their wounded limb. The difference was that the wounded limb was my spirit, my emotions, my whole sense of who I was as a person.

Since there was no point resisting Graham, I just tried to get the sex over with as quickly and painlessly as possible. When it was happening, I would imagine that I wasn't in body anymore. I was somewhere on the ceiling or floating around the room, aware that something terrible was happening but not really to me or my body. This is a skill that every abuse victim learns quickly—to emotionally leave the scene of the crime before the worst happens. It works in the short term, but only later would I learn how much this ability to not be present in my own life would destroy any chance of intimacy with anybody, especially with the people who really wanted to help me.

When I got back from Winnipeg, I was a different person. I had gone to Winnipeg as a goofy, slightly mixed-up kid dreaming about the future and came back as a zombie. I couldn't find words to describe what had happened to me. I also had no idea how my family would react if I told them what had happened. Nothing in my experience could have prepared me to understand the abuse or the terrible emotions it left in its wake. I'd never had sex with a girl my own age, and now I had been to bed with a grown man more times than I wanted to remember. I felt set apart from everything, trapped in a world where my only companion was an awful secret that was slowly crushing me.

It's hard to say what my mom and dad would have done if I'd told them. I know they would have protected me as best they could. They certainly wouldn't have let Graham near me again. Knowing Dad's bad temper, he would probably have done something terrible to Graham, but it was partially my fear of my father that made it so hard for me to tell anybody. I was afraid that Dad would be ashamed of me. I was afraid of looking weak in his eyes. I was afraid that he would somehow blame me for bringing this shame on myself and the family by not being strong enough to resist.

I was plagued by all kinds of irrational fears. Did the fact that Graham chose me mean that I was gay? It was obvious that he wasn't giving this special attention to the other boys, so why had he chosen me? He knew so much about people and the way the world worked, maybe he had seen something in me that I wasn't able to admit to myself. I'd never had sex with a girl, so I had nothing to compare my experience with. Maybe I really had enjoyed the sex but couldn't admit it to myself. And by saying no to one form of sex but allowing another to happen, was I really showing a preference and therefore giving Graham my consent? This is what sex abuse does to a young person: it makes them question everything. The worst part is that this questioning and self-loathing and doubt happens in total isolation and loneliness.

Now that I was away from Graham, I felt dis-

My usual nervous teenage self before a game.

tanced from the abuse somehow, almost as if it had happened to someone else. Life around me seemed so normal. I got up in the morning just like before and did my chores and went to school. I came home, did more chores, and played hockey with my friends. But my shattered emotions kept reminding me that there was something wrong with me, that I was different from everybody else in a way I couldn't describe. There seemed to be an invisible wall between me and everything, and the wall was getting thicker every day. After the first incident with Graham, I stopped dreaming about anything but getting out of my own skin. I dreamed about dying. I dreamed about how I could get out of this world without people thinking that I killed myself. I was shattered.

I don't know if my parents noticed the change in me. When I wasn't working, I would wander off to be on my own or take my motorbike over to a friend's farm. My parents were used to me acting out and going off on my own, so they probably just wrote off my withdrawn silence as another of Sheldon's moods. There was also a big farm to run and 160 cows to milk twice a day. We didn't have time to worry about how we are all feeling on any particular day. That's life on a farm.

It wasn't long before Graham began courting my parents again. He told them how much he loved having me in Winnipeg and how I'd impressed him as a person and a player. I could see that my parents were proud that this powerful, charismatic, junior-league powerbroker was taking such an interest in their son. I didn't know what to do. The more Graham insinuated himself deeper into my life, the more helpless I felt to do anything to stop him. He seemed to always be three steps ahead of me, anticipating people's reactions, saying the right things to the right people, somehow knowing that he could keep people from suspecting him of anything.

Later, after he became my coach, Graham even came out to the farm with me on a few occasions. My parents didn't seem to think it was strange that he asked to sleep in the finished basement where I slept in one of the spare beds. In the middle of the night, he would come for me as he had in his Winnipeg apartment. He would abuse me while I lay there pretending that I was knocked out or asleep or somewhere else. Then he'd go back to his bed. The next day, he sat down to breakfast with my family, acting as if everything was normal. I was in total shock. If Graham could get away with this in my own house, with my parents sleeping upstairs, then there was nothing he couldn't do to me.

Years later, my mother said that she couldn't have believed at the time that Graham would use his power and trust to abuse a defenceless child. But serial pedophiles like Graham prey on the trust and kindness of decent hard-working people like my mother. Where I come from, child molesters are from out of town. They are dirty old men haunting schoolyards, waiting to pounce on the first child who gets separated from the pack. Regular folks can't believe that a respected member of their own community could be carrying on a double life as sexual monster.

In 1984, the Winnipeg Warriors were bought by the town of Moose Jaw, which meant that the new Moose Jaw Warriors owned the junior rights to me and Troy. Graham was still coaching the Warriors, and he arranged for me and Troy to move to Moose Jaw. I would play for the local AAA midget team as well as playing a dozen or more games for the Warriors. This was the opportunity Troy and I had been waiting for since we were kids. We would be players in the WHL, one tier beneath the NHL, with a chance to be seen by the pro scouts who decided who was drafted and who was passed over.

So my parents put us on a bus to Moose Jaw. By that point, I was in such a detached state that I no longer connected what was happening to me in the real world to what I was feeling inside. There was no point trying to control what was happening to me or to the people around me. I had been shown that people who were stronger than you could do whatever they wanted and get away with it. I retreated deeper into myself. Whatever happened, happened.

Troy and I were separated when we got to Moose Jaw. He went off to stay with one family, while I was billetted with Joe and Arlene Dessert, a local couple who were fans of the team. I stayed in the Dessert's basement with two other players. This was a pretty standard arrangement for junior players who'd been sent to play for a team far from their hometowns. Local families connected to the town's junior team billet players and provide them with a homelike atmosphere during the school year and hockey season. They try to keep the players on a schedule and see that they get their homework done.

The Desserts were, technically speaking, my legal guardians, but practically speaking, it is the coach who controls a player's life. In junior hockey, your coach is like a god. He tells you when and how you play, who you play with, who you can talk to outside of the team. He can call up your parents, your teachers, your guidance counsellor, and the police and tell them whatever he wants about you. A coach can ground a player for bad behaviour or failure to keep up in school. If a player gets into trouble with the police or other members of the community, it is the coach who acts as a mediator between the two parties. The coach regularly speaks to the players' parents, reporting on their progress and behaviour on and off the ice. The coach even has the power to send a player home to their parents. If this happens, you might as well kiss your pro career goodbye. Minor league hockey in Canada is a tight, closed community of men who have worked and played together, often for decades. If one of the fraternity decides that a player is "difficult," soon everyone in the league knows.

This structure gives coaches an enormous amount of power over the destinies of young players who are already in an emotionally vulnerable position. Look behind the bravado of a bunch of junior players and what you'll often see is a bunch of scared kids who've been sent away from tightly knit families and communities. They are away from home for the first time in their lives and they are expected to keep up their grades, be responsible members of the communities they've been thrown into overnight, and perform like gladiators in front of thousands of passionate hockey fans. The teams that they play for are also privately owned businesses that are expected to make a profit, which puts tremendous pressure on coaches to get the best performances out of their players and do whatever is necessary to win.

This structure makes Canadian junior hockey somewhat unique. Most junior sporting leagues in North America and Europe are run through schools or local community organizations, which allows the teenage players to live at home and attend school with their friends while pursuing a career in pro sports. When the player graduates from high school, they enter into a junior league or a college sports system. This means that aspiring basketball, baseball, and football players usually live at home until the age of eighteen. (The same is true of hockey players in Europe, although more and more of them are coming here to play in the Canadian junior system.)

The Canadian system is not necessarily better or worse than others, but what people need to come to grips with is that it is the perfect breeding ground for the kind of abuse that happened to me and God knows how many other junior players. Coaches have a tremendous amount of power over a young player's life. The player is often lonely and confused and trying desperately hard to be accepted by his new teammates and coaches. He just wants to fit in and be liked. A coach or manager or team owner or billeting parent can exploit a player's insecurity and inexperience to make them do things they are not comfortable with. And unless the player has a very good relationship with their family or someone in their community, they have no one with whom they can discuss what is happening to them and no one to give them advice or help. They also know that if they complain, they can be sent home or blacklisted.

So there I was, away from home for the first time in my life, under the care of a man who was sexually abusive. He had arranged everything so that he was effectively in control of my life and my career. I had barely set foot in Moose Jaw before Graham started abusing me again. I'd never done well in school, so Graham volunteered to tutor me twice a week at his apartment. Every Tuesday and Thursday night, I went over to his place after dinner to be "tutored."

Whenever I arrived at his apartment, my first thought was to get the sex over with. I knew that there was no way I was getting out of there without giving in to him, so it was best to just get it done as quickly and painlessly as possible. If I resisted, he would chase me around the apartment and threaten to take my privileges away and send me home to my parents, effectively ending my hockey career. When that didn't work, he threatened to hurt me. He was also constantly threatening to tell people that I was gay and that I had tried to have sex with him. He made it quite clear that if I didn't give into his demands, he would go out of his way to ruin my hockey career any way he could. I once told him that I had been abused by one of my teachers, thinking that this might stop him from abusing me. He didn't even blink an eye when I told him. Graham was also very nice to me at times. He would rent videos for us to watch and buy me all kinds of snacks. He also spent a lot of time flattering me about my looks and my hockey skills. Those visits to Graham's were like spending an evening with Dr. Jekyll and Mr. Hyde—he could switch from one person to the other in a heartbeat.

I tried to get out of going to Graham's apartment. He would phone the Desserts after dinner on Tuesdays and Thursdays and I would beg Arlene to lie for me and tell Graham that I wasn't there or that I was sick, but she would say, "Sorry, Sheldon, I can't do that for you." She figured that I was just having a bad day and didn't want to deal with Graham, or that I was just being a typically moody teenager who wanted to hang out in front of the TV with his buddies instead of keeping up with his responsibilities. I would beg her to lie for me but she wouldn't do it. Sometimes I was even reduced to tears but I would eventually just give up and visit Graham's.

I had started living pretty recklessly at that point. I was pounding the drinks back before the age of fifteen, drinking hard. Many doctors now believe that alcoholism is a disease, and I've often wondered if I would have drank as much as I did if I hadn't met Graham. I don't think I would have; neither of my parents were alcoholics. Before I met Graham, I didn't have a lot of interest in alcohol but the abuse filled me with so much shame that I didn't feel comfortable in my own skin anymore. I just felt awful all the time, and I discovered that drinking was the only thing that took the pain away. This got me labelled a problem child, a troublemaker who skipped school and broke curfew to go out and drink. Graham took advantage of this situation by making a very public effort to bring me into line. He positioned himself as my saviour, a big-hearted guy who was always willing to give a second chance to his troubled player.

To make matters worse, not long after Troy and I arrived in Moose Jaw, Mom and Dad got divorced and sold the farm. Things had gotten so miserable at home that I believe Mom thought it was probably for the best that Troy and I had left home when we did. I don't blame her thinking this. Dad's anger had gotten out of control. After the divorce, he basically left our lives, so Mom turned to Graham to help keep her troubled son in line and see that I got by in school. She confided in him about Dad's anger and gruff behaviour, especially toward me, and Graham pretended to confide in her, giving her updates on my progress and relapses, letting her know how I was doing. He came across as a guy who was going to save her child from his angry monster of a dad and be the father to me that I'd never had. I hadn't felt terribly close to my family before the divorce but now I felt absolutely alone.

Graham used my isolation and bad relationship with my father as a way of getting closer to me and gaining my confidence even while the abuse was escalating. He would even listen patiently as I explained to him how my dad had made me feel my whole life, and then he would give me advice on my feelings. I talked to him about these things because there wasn't anyone else who would listen. In return, he played on my insecurities about my father like a master playing the piano. He undermined my confidence and threatened to send me home if I told anyone what was going on. And since Graham had everybody convinced that he was a great guy who was trying to help a family with their troubled son, I figured no one would believe me even if I did tell them what he was doing to me. I had already started acting out by drinking and getting into trouble, so people believed that I was a problem child. No one suspected that Graham was the problem.

After that nightmare year ended, I went home to stay with my mother, who was still living in Elkhorn. That summer, Graham suddenly left the Moose Jaw organization. At the time we didn't know why he had left. What really happened, as we found out over ten years later after the story of Graham's abuse broke in the media, was that James Trapp, the Warriors' general manager, had begun to suspect that there was something wrong with the team's star coach. In August of that year, Graham told James that he was going to Minneapolis with a couple of friends to take in a baseball game. James later found out that Graham had actually gone to the game with a couple of players from the team. James confronted Graham and accused him of lying. Graham said that what he had done was perfectly harmless.

James wasn't convinced. He knew that there was something inappropriate about Graham's behaviour but he couldn't prove that he done anything worse than lie to him about the trip. "My antennae went up that day," James said in an interview years later, "Something just didn't sit right with me…. I didn't want to be around [Graham]. I wanted nothing to do with him" (Laura Robinson, *Crossing the Line* [Toronto: McClelland & Stewart, 1998], 159). James was so suspicious of Graham's behaviour that he went to the team's board and said that if they didn't fire Graham, he would resign as general manager. The board agreed, though many people were angry at James for getting rid of the team's popular coach. If more people had questioned Graham's behaviour, he would never have gotten away with what he did for so long.

My family didn't know any of this at the time. Graham was still in regular contact with my mother, asking her how she was holding up and how I was doing. He was too good a coach to be out of work for long. In the fall of that year, Graham was hired to coach the Winnipeg South Blues, a team in the Manitoba Junior Hockey League (MJHL). The league is one tier below the WHL, with many of the players on their way to hockey scholarships in the Canadian and American universities.

I was still scheduled to play in Moose Jaw the next year but Graham began trying to convince my parents that I should go and live with him and play for the South Blues. My parents argued that playing in the MJHL would be a step down for me but Graham told them that it was still an elite league and that with him personally coaching me my play would still progress. He also told them—and anyone else who would listen—that James Trapp had gotten him fired because he had it in for him and that it would only be a matter of time before he got another job in the WHL. When he did, he would make sure that I was playing on that team.

My parents reluctantly went along with him. I moved down to Winnipeg at the end of the summer into Graham's apartment. This meant that I wouldn't be playing with Troy anymore, which meant one less person for me to confide in. Graham's power over my life was now complete.

That year was another nightmare. The abuse continued as before. My school attendance was spotty at best and my grades even worse. I was drinking even more. I was already carrying a load of shame and guilt and fear from my father. On top of that I had the continuing abuse from Graham. Now I had the shame that comes with alcohol, the shame you feel because now you are wrecking your own life. You have taken on the role of self-abuser. I no longer believed that I deserved anything good in my life, so it was natural for me to sabotage whatever good did come my way.

I was in such a state of shock that I don't remember a lot about playing in Winnipeg. One of my teammates in Winnipeg was Eddie Belfour. He was twenty the year we picked him up for the playoffs. His plan at the time was to quit hockey that year and go back and work on the family farm. The next thing we knew, he was winning the Hoby Baker Trophy.

I was in such bad shape that I dropped out of school and went back to live with Mom, who schooled me herself for the rest of the year. Graham, still playing the role of caring mentor, would regularly drive out to Elkhorn to see me. He needed to keep his spell over me in case I began to talk about what he was doing to me.

From there, I was traded to went to the Brandon Wheat Kings in the WHL, but never played a game with that team. In the meantime, Graham had been hired to coach a new WHL team, the Swift Current Broncos in Saskatchewan, that had moved from Lethbridge, Alberta. Graham immediately began trying to get me traded to the Broncos. The Brandon team valued me too much to trade me, but Graham began working on my mind, convincing me that I needed to play for Swift Current, which he claimed was a better team. By this point he had so eroded my confidence that I believed him when he told me again and again that without his coaching skills I would never become an NHL player. He eventually convinced me to write a letter to the Brandon management asking them to trade me to Swift Current. They didn't want me to go but I continuously lobbied to be traded. Eventually, they allowed the trade to happen.

Before I knew it, I was on a bus to Swift Current. That little Saskatchewan town would be the site of my greatest hockey triumphs. And it would be there that Graham's love for me would explode into an obsession that would consume both of our lives for the next three years.

Chapter Three

Graham was very excited to see me when I got to Swift Current, and not just for the usual reasons. He had been appointed coach and general manager of the WHL's newest franchise and he'd been given almost total control to build the team from the bottom up. He had made it clear to the team's board that he was going to do things his way. He was going to put together a skilled, mobile hockey team that emphasized creativity, puck control, and speed. This philosophy went against the grain of a lot of WHL teams, who were built as much on size, toughness, and rigid defensive systems as skill. He still had a lot of people to win over, and bringing in an offensively talented player like myself was a real coup for him.

The Swift Current Broncos were not technically a new team and they were not really the town's first WHL franchise. The original Broncos had formed in 1966, the same year as the formation of the WHL, but the team moved to Lethbridge, Alberta in 1974. The Broncos then became a Tier II team in the Saskatchewan Junior Hockey League but the town had gotten a taste for major junior hockey and wanted to get a WHL franchise back. In 1982, a group headed by John Rittinger sold shares to over 150 businesses and individuals in town and began courting the WHL for a franchise. It took four years of wheeling and dealing, but in 1986, the Broncos organization bought the franchise from Lethbridge, where the team had moved twelve years earlier. With so many shareholders, the new franchise was effectively owned by the town of Swift Current. That's certainly how most of the townsfolk saw it. Say something bad about the team and you were saying something bad about Swift Current.

Graham had a lot to prove to the thousands of hardcore fans who were pumped for their first season of WHL hockey in over a decade. He certainly didn't make it easy on himself. Graham did not look, talk, or act like your typical, macho hockey coach. He'd never been much of a player, so he could not draw on the instant respect that is given to ex-professional players. He was on the chubby side and had chronic asthma. He was educated, well-spoken, and known for his unorthodox coaching techniques, and here he was going around town promising to get results from an unproven team that did not, at least on paper, seem to be very tough. People thought the team was going to get slaughtered.

Graham really turned heads when he told the board that he did not want the team to accept sponsorship money from any of the beer companies. Sponsoring pro and junior hockey teams is a common practice for breweries across Canada. Almost every junior team in the country receives some kind of backing from a brewery, but Graham insisted that taking money from a company that sells alcohol sent the wrong message to the players, many of whom were too young to drink. So who did he get to replace the beer companies? Yup, a local dairy. The Swift Current Broncos were going to be the only team in the WHL whose official team drink was milk. You can imagine how well that went over, especially with the players, who were going to have to go out on the ice and be taunted by the other teams and their supporters.

So Graham not only needed me in town to be his unwilling sexual partner, he needed me to perform on the ice. He especially needed me to rack up some goals for his new team. Of the ten scoring leaders on the old Lethbridge team, only three remained in Swift Current at the beginning of the 1986-87 season, and two of those would be traded by the 20-game point of the season. The rest had either moved to other WHL teams when the franchise left Lethbridge or been traded by Graham. He was letting everyone in the town and the WHL know that the Broncos were his team and they were going to win his way. If the team did well, his career would take off.

My new billet parents were Frank and Colleen McBean, a well-known and well-liked couple. Frank was a lawyer and one of the part-owners of the Broncos and Colleen was the guidance counsellor at the high school. Not long before I arrived, the McBean's had lost two of their teenage sons in a terrible car accident. Their two surviving children had suggested to their parents that taking in a couple of Broncos players would help them through the grieving process. The McBeans agreed. There was still a lot of sadness in the house but the family seemed glad to have an older teenage boy around.

It didn't take me long to realize that my reputation as a "troubled youth" had followed me to Swift Current. Even before I came to the town, Graham had been talking to people about my emotional problems and my battle with the bottle. And at this point, I had really only just begun abusing alcohol. Graham did everything in his power to put this image of me in everybody's minds, since having everyone worried about my life gave him even more power over me. As long as everybody thought that I was a drunken teenager with emotional problems, Graham could play the part of the good guy who was just trying to help out a messed-up kid.

I quickly began living up to my reputation. I was cutting classes and breaking curfew and finding new drinking buddies in no time. None of this might have happened if I hadn't been forced back into my Tuesday and Thursday night routine of going over to Graham's house for special tutoring. I tried to get the McBeans to stop the sessions but since I wouldn't tell them why I didn't want to go, they didn't do anything to keep me with them on those nights. I would sulk and get angry as I had back in Moose Jaw but by this point, there didn't seem to be any way of stopping Graham. I would go to his house, watch videos, talk hockey, eat dinner, and then Graham would molest me.

Although I didn't tell the McBeans what was going on, they must have known that something wasn't above boards. I don't know what they thought when they heard me stumbling home at five in the morning after spending the night doing "homework" with Graham. He must have convinced them I was so close to going over the edge that any interference from them would be dangerous. He also told them that I was leaving his house on time but finding ways of getting myself into trouble on the way back to the McBeans'.

The McBeans did ask me why I had so much trouble sleeping. I couldn't tell them that nights were the worse time for me. When I was at Graham's, he would have the blinds drawn and he'd be crawling around the apartment. I never knew when he was going to crawl into bed with me. I would hear a noise in the dark and suddenly his hands would be on me. To this day, I still have trouble sleeping at night. I can feel Graham moving out in the dark beyond my bed. I would experience this terror every time I laid down in bed in the dark, which made bedtime something to be avoided, even when I wasn't over at Graham's. I would do anything to avoid going to bed. I realized that if I went out and got drunk enough to almost pass out, then I could stagger back to the McBeans' and just fall into bed. At one point, the McBeans told me that I was drinking too much pop and that all the sugar and caffeine were keeping me awake at night. I don't know how they got this idea since I hardly ever drank pop, and as far as I know, drinking pop does not lead to the emotional problems I was obviously having at that time.

In spite of my inner turmoil, I was making great progess on the ice. The new Swift Current Broncos were having a surprisingly good season, considering how many new and untried players we had on the team. There was no doubt that Graham knew the game of hockey and how to get the best out of his players. He had an eye for talent and loved to draft and trade for players who could play skilled, fast hockey. He encouraged his players to be creative on the ice, to use their special skills and strengths for the good of the team. His teams were exciting to watch. One of the younger players he particularly liked was Joe Sakic, who would go on to rack up 133 points in his first full season in the WHL.

The irony of my success in Swift Current was that not long after the first sexual incident with Graham in Winnipeg, I discovered that, for the most part, my love for the game disappeared. I could still perform like a star on the ice on most nights, but inside me, everything was disconnected and wacko. I didn't like hockey anymore but I didn't know how to quit the game. Hockey had become yet another obligation, another stage where I had to play a part I didn't believe in anymore.

The fans in Swift Current loved my style of play. I was fast and reckless and racked up 68 points in the first season. I got involved in charities and team events and loved going out and promot-

Joe Sakic and I with the gold medals we brought home from Moscow.

ing the team and meeting people, especially kids. I would go into the local schools and talk to the kids about the importance of getting an education and being good citizens. I was always willing to help out in the community. People loved what I was doing for the town and the team, and at the end of the year, I was voted fan favourite, an honour I would win for the next two seasons as well.

I enjoyed being with my new teammates but it didn't take them long to figure out that there was a special bond between me and Graham. They probably knew that he had handpicked me for the team and arranged for me to be traded from Brandon. There were also plenty of rumours about Graham's sexuality floating around the league. It was an "open secret" that he was gay but most people either accepted his sexual orientation or just looked the other way. But I knew there were other rumours circulating about his strange attachments to certain players on his teams. Obviously, nobody put two and two together but there were whispers that he was a bit of a pervert.

Before anybody could really start asking questions, though, the Swift Current team suffered a terrible tragedy on December 30, 1986, when our team bus was involved in a crash that killed four of the players. It was just after the Christmas break and we were on our way to Regina for a game. The bus hit a patch of black ice on the road and went out of control. Suddenly, the bus started moving sideways toward the ditch. The driver tried to get the bus under control by pulling back onto the road but we hit the guardrail. There was a terrible sound of impact from the back of the bus and then we were airborne. The bus flew about 40 feet through the air, landed on its side, and went skidding through the ditch by the side of the road. I was sitting next to Joe Sakic, and luckily neither of us were hurt. The players who died or were injured were all sitting at the back, where the bus had hit the guardrail with enough force to break the players' necks. Two of the players were caught under the bus and two were thrown through the window. It was awful.

When the bus finally came to a stop, we all lay there in shock. It was strangely quiet for a little while. We were bumped and bruised and hurting but none of us could really figure out what had happened. The front windows were disintegrated, so those of us who could walk filed out of the bus through the windows. People had already stopped their cars and began to gather outside. Some of them helped the players out of the bus. Some of the people on the bus were too hurt to be moved, so the bystanders did what they could to make them feel better until the ambulances arrived. Those of us who'd managed to get out of the bus were standing in our sweatshirts by the side of the highway in the thick of a Prairie winter, snow up to our knees, wearing nothing but our socks, too shocked to even care.

We were all taken to the hospital to be checked out and that's when we began to realize just how terrible the accident was. Four players at the back of the bus—Trent Kresse, Scott Kruger, Brent Ruff, and Chris Mantyka—were playing cards when the crash occurred. We found out at the hospital that they were all dead. One of the trainers had a broken pelvis and would need surgery. One of the dead players had a fiancée who would need to be told. Another had two brothers on the team and an uncle who was the assistant coach.

Soon there were parents and relatives and friends and girlfriends phoning up and crowding into the hospital. As soon as they saw one of us, they began asking where their loved ones were. If the person they were asking after was okay, we gladly passed on the news. None of us wanted to be the one to break the news about the four dead players. When people asked about the dead, we looked away or pretended we didn't know, but they could read in our faces what had happened.

You would have thought that someone in charge would have arranged for the survivors to receive therapy to help them deal with the shock and grief following the accident but none of us received any kind of professional help. Nobody seemed to want to talk about what had happened. We were given two weeks off and we all attended the funeral, where Graham gave a stirring speech about the need to move on and to forge even stronger team and community bonds. He said that the Broncos were known as a comeback team and that we would come back from this, our biggest challenge. The thousands of people at the funeral were moved and impressed by his words.

Eventually, the jersey numbers of the four players killed in the accident were retired by the Broncos and a patch honouring the memory of the players was designed that every Swift Current player wears on their jersey. Since 1994, the WHL player of the year is awarded the Four Broncos Memorial Trophy.

So how did we deal with the tragedy? We got back to our lives and tried to move on. We played hockey. And, as men are prone to do, we drank. Only after a few beers, or more than a few, could we talk about how the crash made us feel. Some of us wondered why we had survived while others died. We were plagued by a lot of *what if*s. What if we'd been sitting at the back of the bus? What if the front or the side of the bus had struck the guardrail instead of the back? We all felt lucky to still be alive but we also felt terrible guilt at times, especially when we had to see the families that had lost one of their own. We had no idea what to do with those confusing feelings.

Graham certainly didn't want anyone of the players in therapy—who knows what we might start talking about. He didn't want any of us to let the cat out of the bag about his strange attachment to one of his star players. In private, Graham told me repeatedly that if I had died in the accident, he wouldn't have been able to go on living without me.

The accident only made the people of the town love us more. They rallied around us and tried even harder to make us feel at home in the community. Even the fans in other towns were kind to us. We were given standing ovations in every rink we played in and the team overcame the tragedy and qualified for the playoffs. What this meant for me was that a lot of people thought that some of my reckless behaviour and mood swings were exaggerated by the accident and that the best thing to do was to give me time to grieve and heal.

Over the next three years, Graham's need to be with me became an almost religious thing for him. He was always there by my side, watching me, criticizing me, flattering me, second-guessing me, trying to make me love him and be dependent on him. He took me with him on scouting trips and vacations. Graham completely ingrained himself into my life until he became my life. He was my mother and father and siblings all rolled into one. People didn't phone me to ask how I was doing, they went through Graham. He drove everybody out of my life so that anyone who wanted to get to me had to go through him first. He confided in me about his problems and worries. I was seventeen years old and I had to be a psychiatrist to a pedophile. He used to justify his behaviour to me by saying that as a gay man in junior hockey, he could never just go out and get himself a boyfriend and walk around in public with him. He wasn't keeping our relationship a secret because he was doing something wrong, it was just a way of protecting his career—and mine.

Sometimes I think that Graham actually convinced himself that he was helping me by taking me away and showing me a new life, the kind of life that he loved living. Maybe he really did dream that one day I would become his life partner. But then I think about all the other boys that he preyed on and I remember that Graham is incapable of considering another person's feelings. He wanted me under his power and he was willing to exploit any weakness in me and my family to get what he wanted.

I felt powerless against his efforts. The longer a person is abused, the more they begin to believe that the abuse must be their fault, that they must have done something or there must be something inside them that brought on the attention; worse, they begin to feel that on some level they must enjoy what's happening to them. How else do you explain to yourself why you haven't turned your abuser in or at least punched him in the face?

Graham did whatever he could to alienate me

from the other players on the team. No one was allowed to get too close to me. Graham was already doing everything in his power to keep my bad-boy image foremost in everybody's mind but he needed to do other things to keep me isolated. If I started developing a close friendship with someone on the team, he traded them. He was afraid that if got close enough to another player, I might confide in them about the real causes for my self-destructive behaviour, or even worse, they might even witness something happening between me and Graham. He had to protect his secret.

Graham was intensely jealous of *any* relationships I had outside of ours, and not just because he was afraid I would tell on him. He wanted me to be his little wife, totally dependent on him for everything, including companionship. In his sick way, he wanted me to love him as much he loved me and he didn't care what he had to do to make that happen, even if it meant cutting me off from every other emotional relationship. It wasn't enough that he had control over my finances, my reputation, and my hockey career, he wanted to control my emotional life as well. This is why he was constantly phoning my mother and people who knew me back home to tell them stories about all the trouble I was getting into and how bad my attitude had gotten. If I hadn't gotten into trouble lately, he just made up stories about me.

All that time, he worked very hard to convince me that I would never make it into the NHL without his help. Although I had stopped enjoying the game, hockey was all I had. It was what I was good at and known for. It would have been especially hard for me to walk away from hockey after I'd gotten used to being known as one of the best young players in Canada, a country that loves hockey more than anything. I'd become used to winning and being the centre of attention and being loved by the fans and respected by my teammates, most of whom were older boys that I looked up to. And how do you go to your buddies and tell them that you want to quit when you're not ready to say anything about *why* you want to quit? Hockey was my life, and the whole town had a lot riding on the team's success. Were they just going to watch me walk away from the game without asking me a lot of questions about why I was leaving? Graham knew all of this and constantly worked on my fears and insecurities.

Graham also used anger to control me. He was constantly losing his temper. If someone parked too close to him at the local mall, he'd throw a shopping cart onto the roof of their car. Someone would park in his spot at his apartment building and he'd let the air out of their tires. On a number of occasions, he jumped onto the ice to argue with refs and had to be physically restrained. He threw our sticks onto the ice when he thought the refs were calling too many penalties against us. And then there was the infamous incident where he did a striptease act behind the bench to protest against a few bad calls. If I talked back to him or tried too hard to stop his advances, he would throw a temper tantrum. When a temper tantrum didn't work, he become physically violent. I would tell Graham that I hated what he was doing to me and he would get angry and start chasing me around the apartment. Once he even stabbed me with a fork. There were times when I literally ran out of his apartment in terror, got into my car, and drove off somewhere to hide. Graham would simply send out a posse of players to find that crazy kid, Sheldon. He was also very good at verbal abuse as he knew how to use words to expose my weak spots. Of course, he knew those weak spots in and out: he had created so many of them.

Whether I wanted to admit it or not, I became wrapped up in Graham's world and the fortunes of the team. I still wanted to make it to the NHL, and the only way to do that was to help Swift Current win. But Graham also drew me deeper into the team's inner workings as time went on and he began to see me as his boyfriend. He would discuss team business with me, complaining about other players or praising their performances, and letting me in on the backroom politics and personalities of the team's board of directors. I often knew the trades that he was planning to make before anybody else in the organization.

By sharing his coaching and management strategies with me, Graham made me feel important, someone singled out for their maturity and trustworthiness. I look back on it now and see that this was just another way for Graham to keep me feeling special. It was also a way of drawing me deeper into his world, because the deeper I got into that world, the less chance there was that I could find my way out and tell someone what was happening. He was bribing me, not with money, but by making me his partner. This made the team executives a little afraid of me because they knew that I was aware of everything that was going on with the team: how they were doing financially, who they were trying to trade for, who they wanted to get rid of. I was over at Graham's from five in the evening to five in the morning, so I asked lots of questions. I was curious, and he told me everything I wanted to know.

But Graham was too smart to leave any loose threads dangling. I knew that in spite of his bravado, he was still worried that someone would find out about me and all of the other boys that he had molested. Besides convincing the prominent people in the communities he worked in that he was an upstanding citizen, Graham also forged close and very publicly affectionate relationships with other players on the team. He would never try to have sex with any of these boys. They were just players that he liked to hang out with. He would take five players to a movie and then out for pizza and then drive them home at the end of the evening. Good clean fun for everybody. The people in the town constantly saw him hanging out with his players, so when he took me—or whatever other boy he was sexually involved with—out somewhere, nobody asked any questions. He would even, on occasion, have other players over to his apartment when I was visiting him. On those occasions, nothing strange ever happened. Everything was above boards. I knew that if I did come forward with any accusations, he could mention all the other kids he'd had over to his apartment, all of whom would testify that nothing inappropriate happened under his care. It would be my word against his, and at that point I knew what my word was worth in town.

But even total control over my life wasn't enough for Graham. Sex with boys and the control that he could exercise over their lives were like a drug to him. Boys were to Graham what alcohol is to the alcoholic. He could never get enough, and the more boys that he got away with molesting, the more he wanted and the more he became convinced he would never get caught. The police estimate that Graham molested 75 to 150 kids who were under his care during his time as a coach, manager, and scout. Many of those players were great talents but almost all of them dropped out of minor hockey before they had a chance to be drafted. Their experiences with Graham just made them want to shut the whole thing down. Once you lose your love of the game there aren't a lot of reasons to go out on the ice every day.

Even while Graham was involved with me, he was preying on more of the players under his care. He began paying me and some of the other players to have sex with girls while he watched from the closet. He would also brag to me about all of the players that he'd "seduced" in the past and tell me in great detail about what sexual acts they liked and didn't like Graham to perform on them. On a few occasions, Graham showed me team photos of other teams in the league and go down the rows saying to me, "He's good looking, he's *really* good looking." The next thing I knew, one of those *really* good looking players would be traded to our team. Some of those players were victimized by Graham, but before I charged him with sexual abuse, I vowed to never reveal the identities of any of the players that Graham admitted to molesting. I have kept that promise.

Graham was very good at picking out his victims. He would feel them out first, looking for weaknesses and insecurities before he made a sexual move on them. He looked into a prospective victim's family situations, looking for boys who didn't have a very solid home, boys whose fathers were angry and had drinking problems. Kids with single moms were on the top of his list of potential victims. Graham usually dealt with the mothers of the players on the team. He rarely spoke to the fathers. The fathers were of no use to him. He wanted to find boys who needed a father figure in their lives, boys who were confused and unsure of their masculinity and needed a man they could trust and confide in. When he found someone in that situation, he swept into their lives like Superman. But what the parents didn't know was that Superman was planning to take their sons into a very dark dungeon and that their sons might never make it out of that dungeon. While he was destroying those boys by filling them full of shame and guilt, he kept up his Superman act with everybody else, playing the role of yet another troubled boy's surrogate father and saviour.

There were times when Graham really did seem to believe he was Superman. His arrogance was astounding. He thought he was smarter than everyone else, that he could get away with anything and get anything he wanted. He could walk into a crowded room with his teenage lover and never believe for a second that he could get caught. He had pulled the wool over everyone's eyes. He was the best minor-league coach in the country and everyone wanted him running their team. This gave him tremendous power in the community, and his ego loved that power. He gained the trust of the community through his work with the team and the local schools. He went into the schools promoting teamwork and clean living. He was always stressing the importance of education to the players. He would say that hockey wasn't enough to get you through life, that you had to get good grades and finish high school and help out your family and community. Graham taught us that our hockey careers would last, at best, a couple of decades but that learning could be a lifelong activity. The irony was that in all the nights I spent in Graham's apartment, I don't ever remember opening a textbook. His public image was that of a smart, committed, caring man who loved the game of hockey and the communities where it was played.

I managed to adjust to the life of a junior hockey player. It's hard to explain to someone who has never played professional hockey how different a player's life is from an ordinary person's. You eat, practice, play, travel, shower, and often sleep in close quarters with your teammates. You travel by bus to a town to play and when you arrive you wait until you are told to get out of your seat and get off the bus. Then you walk into the hotel and wait to be told what room you will be staying in. You are told what time to eat, what time to practice, and what time to be back on the bus to head to the arena. You get used to being told what to do without question. You are in a closed world with its own codes of conduct, but many of those codes, as anyone who has ever watched a hockey game knows, are based on demonstrating your physical and emotional toughness. You learn not to show anyone that you are in pain. If you get injured, you are expected to suck it up and brush off the pain with jokes and bravado. You never show weakness around the other players or your coaches. Doing so will get you labelled a baby.

It seemed impossible in such an atmosphere to talk about what was happening with Graham. The whole town was in love with the team and just wanted us to get better and keep the good times and money flowing. I was afraid that if I told on Graham, I would have been shut up and shoved into the background and sent home, the other players would call me gay and shun me, my hockey career would be finished. Looking back on it now, I believe that many, if not all, of those things would have happened to me. Many people tried to shut me up when I wanted to go public about the abuse when I was thirty years old. I can't imagine what they would have done when I was seventeen.

Since I couldn't do anything about the abuse I just took life one day at a time. Hockey took up a lot of time and gave me something to think about. The Broncos lost in the first round of the playoffs in the first year but we did better than anyone could have expected, especially considering that we had lost four players in the bus accident. The team was a huge success in the community and at the box office. A lot of the games drew over 3,000 fans. There were at least 100 Hockey Hounds volunteering to help sell tickets and promote the team. The players were treated like kings. People said hello to us wherever we went. Women wanted to sleep with us and be our girlfriends. Men wanted to buy us drinks. We were welcome at every party and social function.

The next season was even better for the team.

We finished the season with a 44-26-2 record and made it deep into the playoffs. Joe Sakic set a new team record by scoring 160 points in the regular season and was drafted in the first round by the Quebec Nordiques in the junior draft after the season ended. I ratcheted 117 points of my own and was being touted as one of the best junior players in the country.

The next year, in 1988, I was chosen to play for Canada at the World Junior Championship in Moscow. I was honoured to be chosen to play for my country. There was a tremendous amount of pressure on our team to succeed. The year before, Canada had been disqualified from the tournament after the infamous "Piestany Punch-Up" in Piestany, Czechoslovakia. The incident occurred near the end of a very rough game between Canada and the USSR, the last game of the elimination round. Team Canada was winning the game 4-2 and were on their way to the gold medal game. The Soviet team, already out of medal contention, were taking cheap shots at their opponents. To be fair, the Canadians were meeting them with equally rough play. Then the Canadian and Soviet players, after much brutal stickwork and running at each other, dropped their gloves and began a 20-minute brawl that cleared both benches. With the fight out of control, the officials left the ice and the arena lights were dimmed. The fight continued in the dark.

Both teams were disqualified from the competition. Many Canadian fans complained that the Russians started the fight to keep Canada out of the medal round. A lot of fans, including Don Cherry, were proud that the Canadian players stood up for each other on the ice, while others were ashamed of the violence. Either way, the Canadian team that year expected to regain the country's honour and we were expected to do it on the Russian ice in Moscow.

We had a great team that included Joe Sakic, Eric Desjardins, Trevor Linden, Adam Graves, Theoren Fleury, and Mark Recchi. The real star of the team was our goalie, Jimmy Waite, who was chosen to the Tournament All-Star Team after the tournament ended. The Russians had Sergei Fedorov and Alexander Mogilny on their roster, so we had our work cut out for us. We were a fast, reckless team and played with enthusiasm. We didn't lose a single game in the tournament, though the Finns, who went on to win the bronze medal, held us to a 4-4 tie. We beat the Soviets in the final game to win the gold medal and returned to Canada as heroes.

Meanwhile, back in Swift Current, the Broncos were tearing through the WHL. We had lost Joe

Sakic to the NHL draft but players such as Tim Tisdale and Peter Kasowski helped pick up the slack. We finished the season with a 53-16-1 record, and though I missed about 20 games from an injury, I racked up 106 points as the captain of the team. We then went on to win the 1989 Memorial Cup. Graham was picked by *The Hockey News* as the Hockey Man of the Year. I had been drafted in the fifth round the year before by the Detroit Red Wings, so my future looked pretty bright.

But the whole time in Swift Current, I was in a lot of pain and felt a lot of shame. I dealt with the shame I was feeling by always staying outside of the dark ball of emotions inside me. I developed an extremely outgoing personality and became a guy who loved to talk to everybody and tell stories. Anything to keep everybody's focus away from the real me. The easiest and quickest way to achieve this was by drinking. After just one beer, a big weight seemed to lift off my shoulders. The smartest thing to do next was drink fifteen more!

Drinking for me was a way of running from what was going on inside me. I did not want to be in my own life, and while I was drinking, I could feel for a little while that I was living someone else's life. I didn't care whose life it was because anyone's life had to be better than mine. It was my own version of a disappearing act. I felt so crazy in my head that I didn't care what happened. I wanted to die. All day I would think, *God just get me out of here.* I was driving cars and motorcycles and snowmobiles way too fast and I was driving drunk. I was caught and charged on a few occasions for speeding or driving impaired. I thank God for every one of those charges because after I got caught, I would try to get my drinking under control. Each charge slowed me down just enough to stop me from killing myself, which was my real goal.

There were plenty of people around to help me achieve that goal. People liked drinking with me. I never got into fights. I was the joker, the clown, the life of the party who was willing to get crazier than anybody else in the room. People wanted me to play that role, and after a few drinks, I was more than happy to play it. People laughed at my jokes and wild antics, and for a while, I could escape into Sheldon Kennedy, junior hockey star, one of the few who was going to make it to the NHL. I was very slick. I knew how to crawl out the window silently so as not to wake up the McBeans and I knew where to go find some action. At the same time, people were a little afraid of me because they didn't know what was going to happen next when I was around. I was always ready for anything. No stunt was too crazy or dangerous. I remember a number of people just looking at me and shaking their heads and saying, "Sheldon, you're scaring me, man."

I was one of the town's favourite citizens and yet I can't say that I made a single friend there. There were my teammates and guys I drank with, and there were people I met at events and games, but no one was my friend. Everyone wanted to hang out with me because there were always women around and there was always a good time to be had. When you were out with me, you were in for an adventure. But I trusted no one. There didn't seem to be anyone around who could set me straight on what was happening in my life. How could they, when I couldn't even begin to describe to anyone what I was feeling?

I became convinced that everyone on the team knew what was going on between me and Graham. Looking back on it now, I can see that they did know something was going on but they didn't know what it was or what to do about it. There had been rumours about Graham's behaviour with his players long before I came on the scene, so when people found out that I was going over to his place twice a week, it was just a matter of putting two and two together. It was obvious that Graham and I had a very close relationship. The players could see it whenever we were together. They knew that it wasn't normal for a junior player to openly fight with his coach but that's what Graham and I did on a regular basis. At practice, he would ride me about my play or my attitude and I would shout right back at him. I would even tell him to go fuck himself. No one else on the team was allowed to talk to him like that. They were afraid of becoming the next victim of his legendary temper but I openly disobeyed and disrespected him. I regularly called him a fat fuck in front of the players. On the team bus, I would make everyone laugh with my cruel impersonation of Graham, which consisted of making myself look fat, using a lot of fancy words, and constantly puffing on an imaginary asthma inhaler. Graham was very self-conscious about his weight and I brought it up whenever I could to undermine his authority and make him look stupid in front of the team. It was one of the only ways I felt that I could assert any power over him. Graham knew what I was doing but wouldn't try to stop me. He was afraid that if he confronted me—especially in front of the players—that I might say something to give away our secret.

Since I was the team captain, the other players looked up to me and trusted my authority and my ability to handle any situation. I was the captain of the best team in the WHL, how could I allow anything bad to happen to me? If something weird was happening to me, then I must be okay with it. And since I was so close with Graham, they assumed that I was the quickest way into his good books—and his bad books. No one was about to ask me any suspicious questions about Graham's behaviour and what was going on between us because if I took what they said the wrong way, I might tell Graham and then they could be kicked off the team or traded. They were afraid that I might tell on them if I saw them out after curfew. I don't know how they got this last idea into their head, since I was out after curfew more often than any of them!

It was very easy to believe that the players knew what was going on because it seemed like everyone in the entire league had heard about me and Graham. Players and coaches on other teams constantly accused me of being gay during games. On the ice, I just wanted to forget about Graham but even there I was marked as his property. I was taunted and catcalled. The other coaches would shout, "Hey, it's Graham's girlfriend!" The opposing players called me "faggot" and "Graham's little wife" every chance they got. After news of Graham's abuse became public, everyone in the league acted surprised, as if they'd had no idea what was going on. Well, they sure had acted like they knew what was going on. Everyone seemed to know that I was shacked up with Graham.

People in Swift Current also knew that something horrible was going on in my life. I was missing school and getting into trouble but Graham was always there to bail me out and smooth things over. And when you're the captain of the team that wins the town the Memorial Cup and you play on the World Junior team that wins Canada a gold medal, well, let's just say that people are willing to cut you a little slack. Some of my teachers would ask me what was going on but I would just brush them off. I didn't trust anybody, and increasingly, people didn't trust me. Sometimes I'd walk into a room and everyone would look as though they wished they were somewhere else. They knew instinctively that something terrible was going on, that some kind of black cloud hung over my life. A part of them genuinely wanted to know what was wrong with me. They were genuinely concerned but they were also afraid, and I think that in the end, fear won. People wanted to know, but even more so, they *didn't* want to know. They knew the rumours about Graham. How much they really knew, I can't say, but no one seemed interested in finding out more. He was getting results on the ice, he was saying all the right things to all the right people, and he seemed to be the only thing keeping me from completely doing myself in.

I wish people had asked more questions. There was plenty of evidence that Graham was not who he said he was. Here was this man who went around bragging about his own education and lecturing his players on the importance of staying in school but his star player whom he personally tutored twice a week was flunking out of school. Never mind how bad my marks were, why did I hardly ever go to school? And what was I doing staying at Graham's until 5:30 in the morning? Staying out late and cutting the odd class are a part of most teenagers' lives, but how many kids stay out until dawn and only attend sixty classes in one year? There were years in high school that I didn't even write most of my final exams, but the teachers just looked the other way and gave me passing grades.

Finally, after three years in Swift Current, the nightmare finally seemed to be coming to an end. We had won the Memorial Cup and I had had a very strong year. At the end of the summer, I would be reporting to my first NHL training camp. I wasn't sure if I would earn a spot in the Detroit lineup, but that wasn't important, really. The important thing was that I would be out of the WHL and away from Graham. For the first time since I was fourteen years old, my life and my future would not be controlled by the man who had nearly destroyed me.

At least, that's what I thought.

Chapter Four

I had been working toward making it into the NHL for so long that part of me believed it would be the cure for all my problems. I thought that my feelings of shame and guilt and worthlessness would end when I finally achieved the dream of every Canadian boy who's ever played hockey. Being in the NHL would also mean that Graham would not be able to control my life anymore. He wouldn't be coaching me. He wouldn't be able to arrange for me to be traded to a team that he was coaching. He wouldn't be able to coax me over to his apartment.

It didn't take me long to figure out that this wasn't really true. I had a strong training camp. My new coach, Jacques Demers, was impressed by my speed and puck control. I was only 5'10" and 180 pounds but I played like I was 6'5". I was assigned to Detroit's AHL farm team, the Adirondack Red Wings. The coaches assured me that I would be called up at some point that year, and after about a dozen games in the AHL that's what happened. I got on a plane and headed to

Detroit to make my mark in the NHL.

Stepping onto the ice for my first NHL game on November 18, 1988 was both exciting and strange. The Red Wings were playing Boston in an Original Six matchup that had the crowd buzzing. We did the warm-up skate and soon we were lining up for the national anthem. It was a little like being in a dream. I was thrilled to finally be playing in an NHL game in front of over fifteen thousand fans. I had imagined this so many times as a child that I couldn't believe it was happening. For a few moments I felt total joy as I said to myself, "Holy cow, I made it." At the same time, I felt disconnected from the whole experience, just as I did from every other experience I'd had since I was fourteen. I was very nervous. I wanted to do well and earn a spot on the team. I kept telling myself to just do my best and not make any mistakes.

But then I began worrying whether the opposing players and coaches would taunt me once the game began. Did they know about Graham? Would they start calling me a faggot? Would they start asking me if I was sleeping with my new coach? Luckily, no NHL players or coaches brought up my relationship with Graham but I was still afraid that they might find out about it. I also wondered if they knew about my reputation for being a drunk. I had gotten so used to being treated like a problem child that I couldn't imagine what it would be like to be treated differently.

I did okay that first night and stayed with the team for a couple of months, but I was wrong to think that any of my feelings of shame and guilt would disappear just because I was away from Graham and playing in the NHL. If anything, the negative feelings started getting worse. In spite of the great things that were happening in my career, I couldn't enjoy anything. I watched the other players go out there and enjoy playing the game and then get dressed and go home or out with their buddies. I just couldn't understand how they could be so satisfied and calm with their lives. I was still such a mess inside. I was constantly in a state of shame and panic. I didn't feel like I deserved to be on the same ice as the players around me, even though I knew in my heart that I was as good as most of them.

Over the years, Graham had so convinced me that he was the only man who could keep me in line and coach me and teach me how to be a better hockey player that I had trouble adjusting to my new team and the new league. I had trouble trusting Jacques Demers and his staff, even though they did everything they could to help me. I didn't know how to communicate with them in an appropriate way. When Graham had coached me, I could

My bad self during my days in Detroit.

talk back to him on the ice and openly insult him in front of the other players. This obviously wasn't going to go down very well in the NHL, especially in my rookie season.

The strangest part of my relationship with Graham was that, in spite of its abusiveness, it provided me with a day-to-day emotional structure, a way of functioning in the world. I could vent all of my anger on Graham and never really have to worry about the repercussions. I was in on everything that happened to the team. Graham's behaviour, as crazy as it was, was at least predictable. I also knew that if I screwed up, I'd still have a spot on the team. But in Detroit, I felt like I was completely on my own. I was cut off from everybody and started putting all of my energy into worrying about not making mistakes instead of concentrating on becoming a better player.

I also figured out pretty quickly that Graham was still very much involved in my life. Not only did he call me several times a week, he was often in contact with the team's front office about me. He contacted the coaches to let them know what a troublemaker I was, and then told them that he would do whatever he could to help if I got into trouble again. Talk about a self-fulfilling prophecy. Having Graham back in my life only enflamed my feelings of guilt and shame, which made me drink more than I already had been, which got me into trouble, which convinced my new teammates and coaches that Graham was right about me and that he was the only person who could help with the problem. But in spite of it all, Graham was the only person in the world that I still trusted. This was mostly because I knew that he was the only person who knew my secret and that my secret was safe with him. Of course it was; if he told anybody, his life would be ruined. There was a strange security in knowing that about him and this led to a strange connection between us. This is how the abuse victim sees the world: their perpetrator's hold on their feelings and mind is so strong that they believe their abuser to be their only friend.

My desire to go to the rink every day, which I thought would return when I finally made into the NHL, never did come back. Professional hockey at all levels is incredibly demanding, requiring almost inhuman discipline, motivation, patience, and resistance to stress and pain. If your heart isn't in the game, it's very hard to fake interest. There are dozens of hungry young players in any team's farm system trying to scratch their way into the NHL and they would give just about anything to take your place on the roster. Luckily, I had enough pure talent to earn a spot on the team. I had never done any kind of real conditioning, but I got by.

It was around this time that I smoked pot for the first time in my life. It might sound strange, but in spite of all of the carousing I got up to in minor hockey, I didn't do any drugs until I landed in Detroit. In all my years of partying, no one had ever really tried to get me into drugs. Drugs were not part of the culture in those Prairie towns. After a game, you drank. Alcohol was the drug of choice and no one seemed to think twice about it.

When I smoked my first joint, I was overcome with feelings of relief and relaxation. Pot allowed me to just sit back and escape from the pain inside me. I could feel normal in my own skin for a little while. I began smoking pot every day, on top of my drinking, which was as bad as ever. I never smoked before a game, but after the game, I would spark up a big joint as soon as I could. After that, I would hit the bars with whoever wanted to join me.

I probably could have gotten by like this for a while. There was a new structure to my life—new coaches and players and a new pecking order. The practices and games and travel kept me fairly busy. Unfortunately, the injuries began piling up almost as soon as I got into the NHL. In my first year, I dislocated my shoulder and missed a big chunk of the season. This was the worst thing that could have happened to me. I was injured and living in downtown Detroit. I was lonely, confused, and battling a drinking problem, and I was still being paid—very well—but didn't have anything to spend the money on. I'd never been in a city bigger than Winnipeg in my life, so I was totally unprepared for the pace, temptations, and nightlife of Detroit, especially the nightlife that was available for a Red Wing. The partying got worse after I separated my shoulder. I fell in with a fairly rough crowd. I became the life of the party again, only on a bigger stage. I was so out of control by the end of the season that the Red Wings sent me into rehab that spring.

After I got out of rehab, I returned to Detroit. I hadn't been back long when I broke my arm very badly in a car accident. I was leaving a parking lot one afternoon in the summer and was looking for something in the glove compartment, not fully paying attention to what was ahead of me. This was my typical mental state at the time: distracted and thinking about too many things at once. I hadn't been drinking or smoking pot but I was still a million miles away. My left arm was hanging out of the car window as the car moved forward. I felt a sudden sickening pain in my upper arm, which had struck the concrete post holding the small monitor that read the electronic parking cards. My upper arm was shattered instantly. My tricep muscle was pretty well destroyed, and the doctors had to insert a plate and nineteen pins into my arm to hold everything together. At one point, the doctors thought they might have to amputate my arm. My career was on the line. The doctors were pretty sure that I would never play again.

I was in the hospital for quite a while with not much else to do but think about how bad things had turned out. Besides one visit from Jimmy Devalano and Steve Yzerman, no one from the Red Wings organization came to visit me in the hospital. This was very hard on me. I was a young kid alone in Detroit in the summer and no one in the hockey world seemed to care what was going on, not even Graham. This was just another instance of Graham's total selfishness. If he had any concern for me beyond his own needs, he would have visited me or at least phoned to see how I was doing.

I managed to play the next season but my arm was still very weak, which led to me dislocating my shoulder again during a game. The shoulder healed, but it began to pop out of joint more and more. It got so bad that my shoulder would dislocate when I was reaching into the backseat of my car or putting my equipment on. But I had already missed so many games that I didn't want to have an operation to correct the problem. Eventually, I realized that I would not be able to function properly—never mind play in the NHL—if I didn't get my shoulder looked after. The operation was successful but I missed a large portion of my second season after being sent down to the minors for conditioning.

All of this left me with a lot of free time and not much to do. My arm was being looked after by the training staff, and much of my first two years in Detroit seemed to be spent watching the others guys play and practice while I iced my arm. I hit the bars with the other players but never really enjoyed myself. There were always lots of women around who wanted to be with us because we played for the Red Wings. We called them "cling-ons" because no matter what you did, they wanted to hang out with you. I never got off on bullshitting these women and buying them drinks and taking them home. The whole business made me feel awful. I felt like I was tricking these women into having sex with me. Since I had experienced what it's like to be used for sex, I never felt comfortable trying to hound women into my bed. Strangely enough, the only place I really felt at home was in the strip clubs. I could relate to the strippers somehow. Most of them had a sad story in their lives and had experienced shame and loss. I just wanted to get messed on booze and drugs and hang out with one of the girls. I had a girlfriend during my time in Detroit but I found it impossible to open up to her. I didn't want to let anyone in because eventually I would have explain my behaviour and why I was the way I was, and the only way to do that would be to talk about Graham.

I got off by buying things. I had a Harley and a Corvette and a Yukon truck. At one point I even owned a 30-foot speedboat. I bought any shiny thing that caught my eye, just to feel like a big man and feel better about myself for a little while. The only thing that made me feel better was buying some new toy. This meant that every year at training camp, I was scrambling for money. Sometimes I would just live out of my truck. I wasn't so broke that I couldn't afford a nicer place to live but I felt safe in my truck. No one could get me there. I was safe in my vehicle with the doors locked.

Around Christmas of 1990, my second year in Detroit, I did my first line of coke. It was an even more powerful experience than smoking my first joint. After I did my first line of coke, I realized for the first time in my life that I could actually talk to another human being about my feelings and my opinions. After doing a few lines, I just wanted to sit there and talk all night to anybody who would listen. I didn't care what we talked about, it was just such a relief to hear whole sentences coming out of my mouth instead of just wisecracks or the shortest possible answer to whatever was asked of me. The coke also made me even more paranoid than I already was. I loved to talk when I was on coke but I was afraid to be around too many people. When I was doing coke, I just wanted to hang out all night with one person I trusted.

I moved in with Bob Probert during my third season in Detroit. Probie had just been let back into the league after serving nine months in federal prison for trying to smuggle cocaine across the border at Windsor. The NHL had banned him from the league but reconsidered after he received treatment for his addiction. The Red Wings brass thought that if Probie and I moved in together, we would help each other deal with our addictions and stay out of trouble. To put it mildly: the plan didn't work out that way. Probie and I did become very close and did our best to help each other whenever we could. We understood each other's problems and struggles, and we developed a deep respect for each other as people and hockey players. We watched each other's backs on the ice and in the bars, but we also began partying together whenever and however we could. One of us was always ready to hit the town and blow off some steam, and the only way we knew how to blow off steam was to get very drunk and very high.

Jacques Demers did his best to help me and Probie with our drinking problems. He would tell us about his own father's alcoholism to try and give us some perspective on our lives and to help us realize how bad things could get in time if we didn't get our drinking under control. I can't speak for Probie but I was just not ready to hear any of what Jacques was saying. I knew on some level that giving up drinking and drugs would force me to confront the reasons for my addictions and I was not ready to even consider facing that dark whirlpool of emotions. I continued partying, even after I had to spend fifteen days in jail on an impaired driving charge.

My fourth year in Detroit was my best season in the NHL. I'm not sure why I started performing better on the ice. I managed to avoid any serious injuries. It helped that Probie and I weren't living together anymore but I was still partying as much as ever. I was constantly hungover and sleep-deprived at practice. Maybe it's because I'm a farm boy but I was able to physically function at a high level even when I was treating my body so badly. I scored 30 points that year but I knew I could do better. I was a good third-line player but I knew that I had the skill to play on the first line. I could never put together a consistent enough effort to fulfill my potential. I was a flake. I played with a ton of anger and just went out there and hit a lot of guys. My personal life was a total write-off. If I wasn't creating chaos with my partying, I was creating it by running up bills and pissing people off. I was living in fear of bill collectors but even that was better than having to face the nightmares in my head. Anything was better than that.

I went back into rehab for a month at the end of the fourth season. The doctors there put me on drugs and hooked me up to machines but I was using again shortly after they let me out. I became more secretive about my drug and alcohol use. Everyone in the league knew I had a substance abuse problem. Every time I went into rehab, it was in the papers. It got to the point that I couldn't drink a beer without people giving me funny looks. I had to explain myself every time I had a drink. Even when I wasn't a drunk, I'd had to explain to people why I was drinking. It felt like I'd been labelled a drunk since that first night in Graham's apartment in Winnipeg. This only intensified my feelings of self-loathing and the feeling that I was trapped in some kind of double life. At night, I would don my superhero outfit and skate onto the ice and perform for thousands of fans. A few hours later, I was alone in a bar or strip club trying to drown my feelings in booze and drugs.

Meanwhile, I was hearing all kinds of rumblings out of Swift Current. Players were begging to be traded from the team or to get out of their contracts. I knew that Graham had replaced my role as his lover with at least one new young player. Graham even came to visit me once in Detroit with a player from the Broncos who I'm sure he was abusing. The sight of Graham with one of his young victims nearly made me lose it. I could see the numb shame-filled expression on the boy's face and in a second I knew everything that he was going through. I began to panic. My heart was pounding and my mouth was dry. Everything seemed far away. I found some excuse to get away and avoided them the rest of the time that they were in Detroit. When he got back to Swift Current, Graham called me up. He was very upset. He couldn't understand why I had treated him and his "friend" so shabbily. I didn't even know where to begin. My heart was pounding. I wanted to stop Graham but it was like I was under a spell that kept me from speaking.

Later I heard that one of the players had punched Graham in the dressing room during a game, breaking his nose. Graham had to come out for the third period in his track pants because there was so much blood on his suit. He was getting sloppy. More rumours were circulating around the WHL about his sexual habits. He was charged with assault in Moose Jaw in 1992. People were beginning to catch onto his craziness, but of course no one was willing to do anything to stop him. No one even looked into the allegations of sexual misconduct or punished him for his violent outbursts, but I knew that he would eventually move on to another team when people began asking too many questions. Someone would always be willing to hire Graham if he kept getting results on the ice. It was only a matter of time. What I didn't realize was that we would soon both end up in the same city.

I had run out of second chances in Detroit. It was just a matter of time before I was traded, and in September 1994, after my fifth season, that's just what happened. I was traded to the Winnipeg Jets but was claimed in the waiver draft by the Calgary Flames. Calgary seemed like a good place to end up. I had scored my first NHL goal against the Flames, and playing in Calgary meant that I'd be back in Canada and a little closer to my home province. I had a few cousins in Calgary and a grandmother and uncle living on a farm near the city. There would also be lots of opportunities to get out to the mountains to let off some steam, and I hoped that the nightlife in Calgary would be a little more tame than Detroit's. I wanted more than anything to start living something resembling a normal life but I can't say that I had any real plan to go about doing that. I was still living one day at a time, running from my demons and trying not to go crazy.

Not long after arriving in Calgary, I met someone who would finally change my life for the better. I was out playing pool and having drinks one night with a friend. I shouldn't have even been in Calgary but I had a minor injury and didn't join the Flames for a game in Dallas. My friend introduced me to a beautiful woman named Jana. Strangely enough, Jana shouldn't have been in Calgary that night either. Jana was a model who worked in Japan and Australia but she was in town visiting her family and friends. We hit it off instantly. I could talk to Jana in a way that I hadn't been able to with any other woman. I'd had girlfriends since I was a teenager but I'd never felt close to any of them. I didn't know how to love them or relate to them. I wanted them around but I didn't have much to give in return. I didn't know how to do the simplest things, such as talking and being affectionate.

It was totally different with Jana. I opened up to her as soon as we met. We laughed at each other's jokes. We went out for dinner and watched movies and held hands and talked for hours—all the things I'd never been able to do with a girlfriend. We dated for about seven weeks and then one night I just looked at her and asked her to marry me. It was the craziest thing I'd ever done. She looked at me, and without even thinking said, "Yes, I will."

We flew off to Las Vegas at 6:30 the next morning and were married in the Chapel of Love. We both agreed that weddings are supposed to be for the couple that are getting married and both of us wanted a small quiet wedding just for the two of us. We were back in Calgary by 10:30 that night. We phoned our families to tell them the news the next day. My mother was surprised to say the least, especially since I hadn't even told that I was dating anyone, but she and Jana hit off right away.

I only had a one-year contract with the Flames, so Jana and I rented a house up on Coach Hill that overlooked the city. We bought a summer home on an island on Lake of the Woods in Ontario. I spent that first summer with Jana clearing some of the bush from the two acres of land around the cottage with my chainsaw and Weedwacker. I was up early every morning working with my hands. There were about a dozen kids in the other cottages and I loved joking around with them. Life seemed livable, though I was still struggling with alcohol and drugs. Jana was pregnant and we were both excited about becoming parents. My mother and Jana's parents were even more excited about becoming grandparents. Now that my life with Jana had settled into a routine, I quickly got back into my own routine of partying. I was still weighed down with shame and guilt and self-loathing. But that first year and a half in Calgary was the most stable in my life in many ways. I was no longer going on four-day binges. I was keeping it together on the ice, though I knew that I wasn't playing anywhere near my potential. I was in a loving relationship with a woman, though she still didn't know the terrible secret I was carrying inside me.

I was still in contact with Graham during this time but I felt like I could finally get a handle on our relationship, especially now that I had Jana in my life and some solid ground beneath my feet. Graham hadn't tried anything physical with me in years. When we saw each other or talked on the phone, we never mentioned what had happened between us. I thought I had things under control. I was in such denial about how much Graham had damaged me and was still damaging me that I agreed to become a minor partner in the Calgary Hitmen, the new WHL franchise. Graham was a part-owner, coach, and general manager of the team, which played out of the Saddledome, the same arena as the Flames. The other partners included Joe Sakic, Theoren Fleury, Bret Hart, and Geoff Sanderson. Graham had been bugging me for months to become a partner in the team but I wanted to put as much distance as possible between us. I also knew how persistent he could be when he wanted something, so I agreed to buy a $1000 share in the team. I agreed to visit the team's office but I never went to any of the owners' meetings.

Even with my limited involvement with the team, I began to see Graham more often, especially around the Saddledome. Graham would often show up at the Flames games with two or three of his young players. After the game they would wait outside the dressing room waiting to meet me and the other players that Graham had coached. I could see that the kids were mesmerized by Graham's power and connections. He was showing them how much he could do for their careers. Looking at those poor kids was like looking at myself as a sixteen-year-old. I knew that he was taking those kids out to dinner and to the movies. He had control of their bank accounts. He could decide how many minutes they played every game and how late they could stay out at night. He had control of their lives—and I knew what Graham did with that control.

I couldn't believe what was happening. After spending years trying to escape from Graham's influence, I was suddenly working in the same building with him. Worse, I was being forced to witness him ruining the lives of young boys under his control. I felt powerless to stop him. The only way I could help those boys was to let everybody know what had happened between me and Graham, and there was no way I could do that. All the old fears about what would happen if I went public with the abuse came back to me. I would be shunned. No one would believe me. People would say that I wanted Graham to come on to me. I was convinced that Graham would find some way to turn my accusations to his favour and that he'd come out of it looking like a hero while everybody would be more convinced than ever that I was a drunken crazy troublemaker.

I signed for another season in Calgary but things were beginning to come apart at the seams. I told Graham that I wanted my money back and that I didn't want to have anything to do with the Hitmen. He gave me back the money but it didn't make me feel any better. My anxiety and fear were going through the roof. Jana was in the last few months of her pregnancy. I woke up feeling sick most mornings. I was so anxious that the first thing I often did in the morning was to go into the bathroom and throw up. The only thing that made me feel better was smoking pot. It took away the nausea and the worst of the paranoia.

Our daughter, Ryan, was born on January 12,

1996. This day changed my life forever. I was a father now. I had real responsibilities. I had to think about someone other than myself. I had to think about my future, not just how I was going to get through the next day. Holding Ryan in my arms made me realize that I was connected to the world around me and that I couldn't just keep living in my own dark bubble, but I also had no idea how I was going to get out of that bubble. I wanted to be a good father more than anything but I was walking around with this treasure chest full of dark secrets inside me, and until I opened that chest and let everything out, I would never be able to be that father. Whenever I saw Graham, I was reminded that I wasn't the man I wanted to be. I was paralyzed. I couldn't help myself or the kids who Graham was hurting, so how could I help my baby girl and her mother?

I began to drink and drug myself into a stupor. I was living even further on the edge. I hated playing hockey. I couldn't talk to Jana, and my emotions were so out of control that she couldn't deal with me anymore. I wasn't taking care of myself physically. I wasn't performing on the ice. I was showing up to practices late and hungover. I didn't eat or sleep properly and I didn't come home a lot of nights. Jana was scared. I was not the person that she had married not long ago. My behaviour had never been part of our wedding vows. She wondered if I was going to commit suicide. It could be today, tomorrow, or next week, but she was sure I would do it soon. She tried to get me to talk about what was bothering me but I didn't know where to start. I had lived with these feelings for so long that I didn't even know what it was like to feel differently.

Eventually I broke down. We were in Edmonton for a game but I knew I couldn't play hockey that night. A couple of the Flames players found me weeping by myself in the dressing room. They were supportive and wanted to know what was wrong but I could barely speak. I told the coach that I had to go home. I was in such bad shape when I got back to Calgary that Jana could barely understand what I was saying. I was crying so much that in one night I literally went through an entire box of Kleenex. I was shaking all over. Jana could only sit there and try to imagine how anything could make me feel so horrible.

Then one night I finally told her that I'd been sexually abused by my junior-league hockey coach. Her jaw dropped. "Graham?" she said. I nodded. She couldn't believe it at first. He had been my guardian when I was fourteen years old. He was friends with my mother. He had been to mine and Jana's house. She knew him as a friend of the family. I had been one of the part-owners of the hockey team he was running. But she knew right away that I was telling the truth. Jana was relieved that I had told her what was eating at me but she didn't push me to talk about it. She tried to trust that I would deal with this in my own time. We didn't talk about it for a while.

Meanwhile, the Calgary papers were saying that I'd had a nervous breakdown, that I was a drunk, and that my hockey career was pretty well over. In the late winter of 1996, after the stories about my breakdown had gotten out, Graham phoned the house to ask what was going on. Jana was at the breaking point by now. She'd been watching me fall apart for months and turn into a complete stranger. She knew who had caused me all this pain and here he was phoning her at her own house to ask how I was doing. She was blown away that he could be on the other end of the phone expressing his concern and acting as if he had no idea what was wrong with me.

I was standing on the staircase listening to her on the phone. I knew she was talking to Graham. I heard her say to him, "I *know*." There was a pause, then Jana said, "I know what you did to Sheldon." He must have started justifying himself to her, using all the old excuses about his behaviour, but she kept saying to him: "You were an adult and he was a child. It was wrong. It's illegal." He kept trying to justify his actions and make it sound like we'd had a consensual relationship. She told him he was full of shit. "Graham, there is no justification," she said. "You abused your power and trust; I have nothing else to say to you." Afterward, Jana told me that she would never forget the silence on the other end of the phone when she said, "I *know*." He knew at that moment that he'd been caught, and he soon realized that he wasn't going to be able to weasel his way out of trouble this time.

Jana hung up the phone. When she realized that I had been listening to her the whole time, she looked a little scared. She was afraid that I would be upset or mad. Instead, I thanked her. I told her that she was the first person who'd ever stood up for me and taken my side completely. After that, I was able to talk to Jana about what had happened to me and how to decide what I should do next. It was a relief to be able to voice my fears instead of listening to them drown out all of my other emotions and thoughts. I told Jana that I was afraid no one would believe me if I accused Graham of sexual abuse. She said, "I believe you and *you* believe you. That's all that matters." I told her that I was afraid people would say that I was gay and had wanted to have sex with Graham. I told her that I was afraid my career would be ruined and I would lose my friends. All the fears that Graham had planted in me came out in a big gush but Jana made me realize that those fears didn't make any sense.

Another person who was very supportive at that time was my new agent, Tom Laidlaw. Tom had known about my history of off-ice problems but he had agreed to consider representing me after my old teammate in Detroit, Dallas Drake, recommended me to him. He came to visit Jana and me in Calgary in the spring. During our first meeting, I told him about the abuse and all the struggles I'd had in my life and my career. I was crying. He was crying. He was so shocked that he had to take a nap afterwards but he agreed to represent me. I felt tremendous relief. Tom didn't think I was crazy or a bad seed. He told me that I was very brave to confront the abuse and that he would be proud to be my agent. Maybe Jana was right when she'd told me that I wouldn't be shunned in the hockey world for going public with the abuse. When Jana and I went to the hotel to say goodbye to Tom, I could tell that he felt awkward about touching me. He wanted to respect my emotions and boundaries and wasn't sure how I felt about being touched. Jana saw all of this and just said, "God, why don't you two just hug each other, all right?" We did.

I rejoined the Flames just before the playoffs started and I told the team's management about the abuse. They listened and tried to be sympathetic. They recommended that I go see a hypnotherapist. I did not find the experience useful. The therapist seemed to be interested in one thing: getting me mentally fit enough for a long playoff run with the team. Management and the therapist wanted me to just learn to relax and keep calm. They wanted me to concentrate on scoring goals. Graham's name hardly came up. Although I wanted to do my best for the team, hockey was not at the top of my list of priorities at that time.

Calgary lost four straight games to the Chicago Blackhawks in the first round of the playoffs that spring. After the first loss in Chicago, I was sitting around the hotel room with a few of the players talking and having a few beers. I had wanted to tell my teammates for a long time about the abuse but I could never seem to find the right opportunity. Right in the middle of the conversation, I blurted out that Graham had sexually assaulted me. I told them a bit about what had happened. They were stunned. They did their best to be supportive but none of them really knew what to do or say. Nothing in their lives had prepared them to deal with something like this, but their support proved to me that I wouldn't be shunned by my fellow players when they learned about my secret. This was a tremendous relief for me.

Luckily, my old friend Dean Evaston was in the room that night. We had known each other since we were kids and we used to visit his family every summer for a couple of weeks. After the other guys left, Dean and I went out to a coffee shop for a few hours. He let me get everything off my chest and he believed everything I told him. Since Dean had been in the same junior hockey system as me, he understood how Graham had used his power as a coach to force me into having sex with him. He understood how hard it is to be sent away from your family when you're still a kid. He asked me if I thought that Graham had molested any other boys in Swift Current and I told him that I was sure he had. I also told him that I was sure he was still preying on some of his players in Calgary.

After the season ended, I was without a contract for the next year. I decided to get help from the NHLPA substance abuse program to deal with my drinking and drug problem. Graham had not tried to contact me since he'd spoken to Jana on the phone that day. He knew that time was running out for him. He must have heard that I had told my teammates and management in Calgary about the abuse. But he was still free. I spoke to Jana and she agreed that given Graham's patterns in the past, he had to still be molesting boys. Someone had to stop him. Someone had to stand up to him, no matter what the consequences. It was the only right thing to do. I had to set an example for my daughter, to show her that you have to stand up against evil in this world. Jana and I eventually decided that I would go to the police and formally charge Graham with sexual abuse. It was the only way to stop him from hurting anyone ever again.

Chapter Five

Late that summer, with Jana's support, I phoned the Calgary police to formally charge Graham with sexual abuse. I had so convinced myself that no one would believe me—that Graham had actually done something wrong—that I was a little surprised at how seriously the police considered my complaint. My case was given to Detective Brian Bell, who agreed to meet me at the house of an undisclosed person. I showed up at the house at the appointed time and Brian took my statement.

It took a few meetings to get the whole story out of me. It was hard talking about the abuse to strangers but Brian was patient and respectful. He also brought in some specialists in the field of child abuse to help with the process. Over the course of the interviews, the police concluded that Graham had sexually assaulted me more than 300 times over the years. They also wanted to know if I'd witnessed any acts of sexual abuse on other players. I told them about incidents that I had witnessed, and they began their investigation. They drew up a list of every hockey team that Graham had been involved with since 1982 and began interviewing his former players. The police were pretty sure that they would find more victims willing to come forward and press charges but they couldn't promise anything. I understood. It had taken me almost a decade to press charges, and I'd been lucky enough to have the support of my wife, who had stood by me during all of the struggles. Many of Graham's victims, battling their own intimacy and addiction issues, would not be so lucky.

Knowing that the case was now in police hands gave me my first taste of freedom. I had done everything that I could and now a group of trained professionals were going to do everything they could to bring Graham to justice. The Calgary police set up a Canada-wide investigation of Graham's past. They were sure that there were many other victims, perhaps as many as 100, maybe even more. As horrible as it was for me to think about how many people Graham had hurt over the years, I felt a little less crazy when the police confirmed what I'd known, but could never prove, for a long time: that Graham was a sexual predator who preyed on confused lonely boys.

It didn't take long, though, for the old fears to return. What if I was wrong? What if someone proved that I'd consented to the sex with Graham? What if the police couldn't prove anything that I'd told them? If it was just my word against Graham's, who would the court believe? Who would the media believe? Graham was still widely loved and respected in the hockey world, while I had become a bit of a joke in the NHL. It didn't look good. The next thing I had to do was tell my family and friends. I didn't want them hearing about the charges against Graham and wondering if I was one of his victims. I called my mother. She cried and cried. She said that she'd known for so long that something was bothering me but she couldn't figure out what it was. She felt so awful that she hadn't figured out what had been going on and stopped it, but I explained to her that she wasn't the only person that Graham had fooled. My father just asked, "Why?" Why had Graham done something so horrible to a boy?

I phoned the McBeans in Swift Current. Colleen was devestated. All she could say was, "Of course. It all makes sense now." She couldn't believe that a child in her care had been abused and she hadn't seen what was happening. I called my brother in the middle of the night and told him that I was going to take Graham to court. He asked me why. I said, "Child abuse." He said, "Oh really?" He wasn't surprised, but at the same time, he would never have guessed in a million years what had been going on. He, like everyone else, knew that something terrible had been happening to me, but like everyone else, he had trusted Graham's polished image.

Suddenly, the last twelve years of my life made perfect sense to everybody who loved me. All the drinking and drugs and self-abuse and silence. All the acting out, the anger, how I couldn't look anybody in the eyes when I spoke to them. Everyone understood why I had been such a mess for over a decade. I understood too, but I was still a mess inside, full of irrational fears and anxiety. Telling Jana and my family and friends had relieved some of the pressure but not all of it. I just prayed that I would have the strength to continue working with the police and go through with my vow to put Graham behind bars and prevent him from abusing a child ever again.

Meanwhile, I was still fighting my old addiction problems. I was receiving counselling through the NHLPA but I found it next to impossible to get through the day without smoking pot and having at least a couple of drinks. Tom Laidlaw had gotten me a one-year contract with the Boston Bruins, so I had a place to play for the 1996-97 season, but I was in no shape for training camp. Tom and the NHLPA arranged for me to miss training camp that year. The official line was that I was missing time for "personal reasons," but I knew what people would be thinking: Sheldon's back on the bottle again. But Tom and Jana assured me again and again that I was doing the right thing and that was all that mattered.

The police were following up on many leads when the worst possible thing happened. On September 7, 1996, the *Calgary Sun* published a story with the headline "City Police investigating former coach." The story reported that popular junior-hockey coach Graham James had resigned from his position as head coach and general manager of the Calgary Hitmen. The reason: he was being investigated by Calgary police for allegations of abuse. One look at the article told me that, as usual, Graham had managed to win everybody's loyalty. Everyone interviewed for the article was shocked and supportive of Graham. One player said, "He was a good coach and we all liked him." The team president said, "Graham was a friend and was looked up to as one of the best coaches in hockey."

My old teammate Tim Tisdale went even further in defending Graham in the article. "I've never seen anything that would make me believe he did anything wrong," he said. "Until there's proof somewhere that convinces me otherwise—which I don't think will be the case—I'll support him." I guess Tim didn't hear all those players and coaches on the

On the ice with my final NHL team, the Boston Bruins.

other teams taunting me for being Graham's little wife. There would be hundreds more testimonies to Graham's character before he was sent to jail. In fact, people would go on defending Graham even after he admitted to molesting me. It was as if people could not believe that the man they had grown to love and respect could possibly be the same man who preyed on vulnerable teenage boys. How could it be? Graham was funny. Graham was smart. Graham knew hockey. He knew how to run a team, chair a meeting, get the best out of his players. He wasn't just a good coach and general manager, he cared about his players. He went out of his way to help them. He sacrificed his time to make them better players and better people. He spoke out against violence and hazing and boozing in junior hockey. Again and again, Graham's defenders would bring up these points to defend his character.

Sometimes Graham's defenders brought these things up because they were having trouble believing that he had fooled them so completely and for so long. That's understandable. We've all been taught to think that sexual offenders are the losers of society—dirty old men in trench coats who are forced to get their kicks by jumping out from behind bushes and snatching up innocent children. If the last twenty-five years of court cases have taught us anything, it's that sexual abusers are often trusted members of the community who are in positions of authority over children. They are the priests at the local church, the coach of the softball team, the camp counsellor, the Boy Scout leader, the choir master, the teacher, the janitor, the father, the babysitter, the grandfather, the uncle or aunt. And what they all have in common is that they have learned to hide their behaviour from the public eye. How else would they get away with what they have done for so long? Most people who look after children would never think of harming them, but until our society accepts that sexual abusers are often their friends and neighbours, we will never do anything to stop this horrible crime. What people have to understand is that it takes a sick kind of sense for child abusers to get themselves into a position where they have access to a wide selection of children. What better way to find new victims than to be put in charge of dozens of vulnerable, impressionable children who are eager to please the authority figures in their lives?

Of course, Graham did everything he could to make himself look like a humble big-hearted guy after the allegations went public. I guess by this point in his life it came naturally to him to play the role of the good guy. When he was interviewed by the *Calgary Sun* on September 9th, he said that no matter how badly he felt about the allegations of abuse, nothing could be worse than the day he'd lost four of his players in a bus crash. "I'll go on living," he said, "That's more than they got." He then said that even the bus crash had not "steeled" him for what the allegations were putting him through and that all of the phone calls of support he'd received were keeping him "half sane."

Another result of the story breaking before the police had finished their investigation was that it made it harder for them to find witnesses and other victims. One of the investigating officers was quoted as saying that as soon as the allegations were leaked by the media, all of the leads the police were working on dried up. "We could just imagine [Graham] on the phone calling up all the victims and telling them not to talk," the officer said (Robinson, *Crossing the Line*, 154). It began to look like I might have to go it alone against Graham, my word against his.

Luckily the police did find one victim who was willing to come forward. I can remember the tremendous relief I felt when one of the detectives phoned to tell me that another ex-player of Graham's would also be pressing sexual abuse charges. The victim told almost the exact same story as mine, right down to the shotgun in the closet. Knowing that I wasn't alone gave me a little bit more freedom from my fears. I wouldn't be alone. No one could say that I had made the whole thing up. For the first time since I'd met him, Graham would be the one who'd have to look down at the floor in embarrassment and shame, not me. For once, I was going to be the one looking up.

Once the hockey season started, the story died down in the media for a while. I was still trying to get myself ready to play for my new team, getting myself in shape physically and mentally. The Bruins management knew why I hadn't come to training camp or the first month of games and were doing their best to be understanding and patient. The NHLPA was protecting me, making sure I got paid and received help for my struggles. To this day, I am thankful for everything they did for me.

I was still a mess on the inside and the outside. I couldn't sleep properly. I was nervous all the time. I had hoped that telling Jana, my family and friends, and the police about the abuse would free me from the shame and guilt and fear, but I was beginning to learn a lesson that would take me years to accept: it takes a lifetime to heal from abuse. I was also learning that when you open up that treasure chest of horrible memories and emotions, your symptoms actually get worse for a little while. You begin to feel all the hurt and shame that you prevented yourself from feeling when the abuse was happening. You relive the abuse as an adult but you still feel like a frightened confused child. It can feel like the pain and the memories are never going to end but I was glad that I had finally done something to end the cycle of self-abuse. I had days where I almost felt human again, especially when I would play with Ryan. She reminded me that children are not born afraid and suspicious and withdrawn. I also realized even then that if I hadn't told Jana and gone to the police, I would have eventually killed myself. Disclosure was a big step, the first of many, but it was proving to be harder than I had thought.

Then, on October 29th, the *Calgary Sun* ran a story with the headline, "Ex-Flame involved: Sheldon Kennedy an alleged victim in James case." Out of respect for privacy, most newspapers do not print the names of sexual assault victims, but I guess the editors at the *Sun* couldn't resist printing their big scoop. I refused to comment when the journalists began to call. I knew it was only a matter of time before someone proved that that I was the player who had pressed charges against Graham, but I wanted as much time as possible to get my hockey career on track and to prepare myself for the trial. There also didn't seem to be any point in trying to get my story out in the papers. Everyone was going to believe Graham anyway. Tom Laidlaw was also contacted by the media but he stuck to our story about me being away from the Bruins for personal reasons.

The police went to arrest Graham on November 22nd. According to Brian Bell, Graham was visibly frightened when he was arrested. "He almost had an odour of fear about him," Brian said. "He didn't want to look anybody in the eye. He looked at the floor. He was very robotic in his movements, dry mouthed. He was shaking. He was fearful of what was going to happen to him next" (Robert Duncan, *Sheldon: A Story of Human Courage* [CTV, 1999]). Brian might have been describing how I had acted for the last twelve years of my life. I joined the Bruins about a month into the season. Hockey provided a nice distraction but I kept thinking about the trial.

On January 2, 1997, Graham appeared in a Calgary courtroom with his lawyer and pleaded guilty to 300 counts of abuse against me and 50 against the other player who had charged him. I missed a game against the Ottawa Senators to be at the hearing, though I had already been told that Graham would plead guilty and that I would not have to testify. On the one hand, I felt relieved that Graham was not going to fight the charges in court. I was not looking forward to standing up in a courtroom and talking about the horrible things he'd done to me, then having his lawyer spend days trying to prove that I was a liar or that I had consented to the sex. I had been in such a fog of pain and alcholism during the years of the abuse that I would probably make mistakes about dates and times when the lawyer questioned me. The lawyer would have picked up on this and tried to discredit me in front of a jury. I had gotten so used to people believing Graham's version of events that I almost believed that a jury would think I was some kind of flake and then find Graham innocent. I also felt relieved because now everybody in the hockey world would hopefully understand some of my crazy behaviour a little better. I didn't want to make excuses for some of the things I'd done but it would be great to make a fresh start.

On a deeper level, I felt tremendous anger that Graham was pleading guilty. If the case had gone to trial, the police and lawyers would have put dozens of people—former players, general managers, hockey executives—on the stand and questioned them about Graham's behaviour. The lawyers would have asked why Graham kept getting shipped from team to team and why none of the suspicions about his close relationship with some of his players was ever looked into. Graham had been fired from a coaching position in 1977 after he was found in a hotel with his players well after curfew. He had also been investigated by the police when he was nineteen for having sex with a thirteen-year-old player. The lawyers would have asked why, if nobody suspected that Graham was having a sexual relationship with one of his players, did so many opposing players and coaches heckle me about it for years. And if the case did go to trial, players who had told police that they had never been victims of Graham, or witnessed him victimizing anybody else, would have had to say so under oath. They would have also been grilled by lawyers about what they had or hadn't seen. I can only wonder how many more of Graham's crimes would have been unearthed if the case had gone to trial. As hard as it would have been on everybody, I still think that the victims—and the North American pro and minor hockey systems— would have benefited by a closer examination of Graham's activities over the years.

I knew, as I sat there in the courtroom waiting, that there was only one reason why Graham was going to plead guilty. It was not out of a sense of moral guilt or responsibility or because he wanted to confess his crimes and try to turn over a new leaf and become a better man. He was going to plead guilty because his lawyer had told him that the evidence against him was too strong. He was going to plead guilty because for once in his life, all of his lying and acting and bullying and flattering would not get him out of trouble. For once in his life he would not be able to whisper lies and innuendo into people's ears to make them blame the victim instead of the perpetrator. This wasn't the old boys' club of junior hockey; this was a courtroom. Graham also knew that if the case did go to trial, the police would likely find many more victims and witnesses to testify against him. So Graham was doing what he always did: taking the chicken-shit way out and cutting his losses.

I knew that Graham still didn't think that he'd done anything wrong. He had tried to justify his behaviour to Jana the day he phoned to ask me how I was doing, and he hadn't apologized or admitted any wrongdoing then, and he hadn't tried to contact me since. Another thing that convinced me that Graham had no remorse for his actions was a made-for-TV script that he had been developing with a production company. One of the film's producers showed me a copy of the script a few months before the abuse allegations broke in the *Calgary Sun*. The film, which was to be produced by the CBC, was called *Broncos*, and it told the heroic story of how Graham took a bunch of untried junior hockey players—including me and Joe Sakic—

and turned them into the team that would go on to win the Memorial Cup. Everything was in there, including the bus crash and a lot of the real players from the Swift Current teams of the mid-1980s.

Graham didn't write the script but he might as well have. It wasn't enough that he made himself look like a great guy who always put his team first and tried to teach his players to be something more than gladiators on skates, he had to do so at my expense by making me look like a drunken clown. The script is full of scenes of me partying, making an ass of myself, and using my looks and position of team captain to bed as many women as I could. It was a perfect portrait of how Graham had been portraying me to people since I was a teenager. Even by Graham's standards, the script wasn't fair to me. I certainly had a drinking problem and I certainly did like to play the team joker but even at my lowest moments in Swift Current, I only ever hurt myself. I was never the sex monster who used women to make himself feel like a man, as I was portrayed in the script. When the CTV movie about my life story later screened at a Vancouver film festival, I was told by one of the producers working on the *Broncos* film that the project had been about a week away from been green-lighted when the abuse allegations appeared in the *Calgary Sun*. So maybe something good did come out of the leak.

Graham looked nervous in the courtroom. He didn't look at anybody, except his lawyer when he had to. He looked like he just wanted to get things over with and see what happened next. Graham's lawyer, Lorne Scott, gave a statement to the court that he asked to be considered in the sentencing. The statement contained many letters of reference from former players and fellow hockey colleagues. Time and time again, Graham was portrayed as an intelligent, trustworthy, loyal coach who had made a positive impact on the communities in which he worked. One former player praised him for never using a bribe or a threat to get the best out of his players. This player went on to say that he had never heard anything bad said about Graham and that he wished he had met more people in his career like his former coach. Another player, who was interviewed by police and knew about the charges, said that in his heart he knew that Graham was "a great coach and a great person" (Robinson, *Crossing the Line*, 167). I wonder what they would think about him when they found out that he had pleaded guilty.

Lorne then tried to convince the judge that Graham was sorry for what he'd done and was pleading guilty to spare his victims the agony of having to tell their story in a trial setting. He said that Graham knew that he had "made a very significant and serious error in judgment in becoming emotionally attached to these men, and in particular, for Mr. Kennedy." A serious error in judgment? That was a bit of an understatement. Lorne then went on to argue that Graham did what he did because he loved me. He said it was not a case of "straight sexual gratification." I was Graham's "great friend" and we had shared a long relationship on and off the ice. Lorne tried to prove this by showing the judge a Christmas card that I had sent to Graham when I played for Detroit but it got even worse. Lorne said that Graham had never physically threatened me or the other player and that the incident with the shotgun was "more of a joke. He never intended to threaten Mr. Kennedy. Mr. Kennedy may have viewed it as a threat, he was fourteen or fifteen at the time." Scott also asked the judge to consider that by the time the "various incidents" ended that the victims were big "nineteen-year-old hockey players ... not little children." Lorne said that he wasn't trying to undermine the seriousness of Graham's crimes but it sure sounded that way to me.

Lorne asked the judge to sentence Graham to three and a half years. He said that Graham was not at risk of reoffending; that he realized what he had done was wrong and had been receiving therapy. According to Graham's psychologist, Graham was not a pedophile but a homosexual who had not understood that he was abusing his position of authority by having sex with his players. The fact that it is illegal to have sex with a fourteen-year-old and that homosexuality, like heterosexuality, has nothing to do with wanting to have sex with teenagers, did not seem to occur to Graham, his lawyer, or his psychologist.

My lawyer disputed some of these facts but the judge agreed that three and a half years was a fair sentence for Graham. He was led away in handcuffs and leg irons and taken to the maximum security penitentiary in Edmonton.

There was a mob of television and newspaper journalists outside the courthouse. I knew that some of them had recognized me and that it was only a matter of time before I would be hounded by reporters asking me why I had appeared at the sentencing. I decided that the next logical step was to speak to the media.

I made arrangements to meet with four journalists the next day at a hotel room. When they arrived I told them that I was one of the two victims who had charged Graham James with sexual assault for incidents that occurred while he was coaching me in minor hockey. I also told them that the other victim did not want his name to be made known to the public. I answered their questions as best as I could. They asked why I had decided to disclose my identity and I told them that by coming forward I might be able to help other sexual assault victims who were still too afraid to tell their stories. If some fifteen-year-old kid who was being abused saw a big tough NHL player coming out in public as an abuse victim, then maybe they would find it easier to tell someone about their abuse. I wanted to open a door for all of the victims out there. I also tried to explain why the abuse had gone on so long and why I had waited so long to press charges, and why I felt that Graham was still in denial about what he'd done.

I flew back to Boston to rejoin the team. I was hoping to put Graham's trial behind me but my interview with the reporters seemed to be printed in every newspaper and read over every TV station. Former teammates of mine were interviewed and expressed shock and support for me. On the popular Coach's Corner segment on *Hockey Night in Canada*, Don Cherry expressed his disgust at Graham's actions and the short prison sentence he'd been given. Don was his usual blunt self, saying that if it was up to him he would have drawn and quartered the son of a bitch. A reporter from ESPN managed to set up a phone interview with Graham from prison. Even from his jail cell, Graham was still trying to make himself look like a good guy. He said that in spite of what had happened, he hoped that he could still be friends with me one day. "As ridiculous and impossible as it sounds, that's how I feel," he said. "You know, I always hope that some day something can be done to bring about a reconciliation" (Duncan, *Sheldon: A Story of Human Courage*). When a reporter asked me what I thought of Graham's comments, I just said, "He doesn't get it. He still thinks it's all right."

My teammates in Boston were very respectful and supportive when I returned to the team. I was given a standing ovation in my first game back with the team, and even the opposing players congratulated me. Not long after, we played a game in Calgary and the fans gave me a long standing ovation. Jana was in the crowd and I knew how proud she was of what I'd done. I had been afraid that if my name got into the papers, I would be shunned or disbelieved, and here were 19,000 people standing up and cheering me. The support of the fans and the players told me that I had made the right decision. It felt good. For so long, I'd felt like I'd been living on the bottom of the ocean, but for a few minutes that night, I felt like my head was finally above water.

I was wrong to think that I would be able to put the court case behind me and focus on my hockey career. As the news of the identity of Graham's accuser spread, I was contacted by newspapers and TV stations all over North America. Everyone seemed to have heard my story and wanted to interview me. I was being called a hero from coast to coast and all stops in between. I was asked to appear on countless radio and TV talk shows, including Rosie O'Donnell and Oprah Winfrey. ABC's *Primetime Live* did a feature on my story. CTV made an hour-long documentary on me and began negotiations to make a movie based on my life story. I agreed to let them make the film but insisted that they allow me to see the script and veto any scenes that I did not think were true to life.

I got so used to telling my story over and over again that I could do it in my sleep. In fact, I felt like I was asleep a lot of the time. I was walking around in a daze, talking to every microphone that was shoved in my face. My pot habit was as bad as ever. I was still waking up so nervous that I felt sick to my stomach. The only way to get rid of the nausea and fear was to smoke a joint, which put me in a fog for the rest of the morning but at least allowed me to function.

Although the journalists and talk-show hosts I spoke to were sympathetic, there was an assumption that since Graham was behind bars and I was dealing with the effects of the abuse, I was therefore healed or at least well on the way to being healed. I certainly wanted to believe that, and in many interviews, I said that I felt better than I had in years. This was partially true. I was having good days, and it was a relief to know that Graham had been punished and could not hurt anyone where he was, but it often felt like I was telling people that I felt better because I wanted it to be true and I wanted people watching me on TV or hearing me on their radio to also believe that it was true. I wanted them to believe that coming forward and naming my abuser had freed me from the worst of my demons. I wanted them to see that coming out as an abuse victim had not destroyed my career and made me an outcast. I knew there were millions of abuse victims out there afraid to speak and I wanted to show them that they didn't have to be afraid anymore. I especially wanted Graham's other victims, many of whom were still playing hockey in various leagues around the world, to know that there lives would not be over if they came forward and charged Graham. I hoped that they would seek some kind of counselling for their suffering, even if they chose not to press charges.

As I said in many interviews at the time, if a victim couldn't handle coming forward, they had to deal with the effects of the abuse in their own lives.

As my story appeared in more and more media outlets, the police, sexual-assault clinics, and various helplines noticed a steep increase in the number of men coming forward with stories of sexual abuse at the hands of hockey coaches. Some of these assaults happened decades earlier, some were still going on. The Calgary Sexual Assault Centre reported that they went from dealing with twenty calls a month from abused men to twenty a week, with 25% of those calls concerning abuse suffered at the hands of hockey coaches. Similar statistics were reported by sexual-assault centres across Canada. As much as the Western and Canadian Hockey Leagues wanted to portray Graham James as a bad apple who had snuck into the squeeky clean world of junior hockey, it was becoming obvious that dozens of sexual predators had infiltrated the Canadian hockey system at every level, preying on vulnerable boys and young men.

What also became obvious was that this story had been swept under the carpet for many years. Complaints had been made about coaches and the complaints ignored or covered up. The father of the other victim who charged Graham was interviewed a couple of days after Graham was sentenced and claimed that his son had gone to the Broncos management three years earlier to complain about the abuse and that nothing was done about it. The Broncos simply let Graham's contract run out and let him go to Calgary. The next day, the victim himself was interviewed by the CBC and confirmed that he had filed a complaint against Graham with the Broncos but that the team did not take the complaint seriously. Graham left him alone after that but he was allowed to continue coaching the team. Then, Gary Bollinger, vice president of the Broncos in 1986, admitted in an interview with the *Calgary Sun* that he had heard Graham and I were having a sexual relationship. He didn't look into the matter but he did question the team's board when Graham decided to take one of his players with him on a scouting trip to Czechoslovakia. He confronted Graham about it but Graham didn't say anything. Shortly after, Bollinger was fired.

About a week after the Bollinger interview, former Broncos player Darren McLean told the CBC that he had been cut from the Broncos for complaining about Graham's behaviour. Darren said that he started hearing about Graham's sexual relationships with players as soon as he joined the team. He said that Graham wasn't doing much to hide his behaviour anymore and that it only seemed a matter of time before someone blew the whistle. The next season was even worse. "Graham wouldn't spend any time with the rest of the players, for the most part he lost interest in us," Darren said. Darren and a couple of other veterans on the team began warning the new young players that Graham had obviously picked them out for special attention. They told the players not to do anything with Graham that made them uncomfortable. Then in February 1994, Graham's "special player" broke Graham's nose in the locker room. That player was the second complainant in the court case against Graham. Darren then went to the team's assistant general manager and told him that Graham was sexually propositioning players and paying players to have sex with girls in his basement while he watched.

A team meeting was held with the assistant general manager, who brought the complaints to the team president, John Rittinger. John agreed that Graham should be relieved of his duties, but at the rink the next day, Graham spoke to the team and singled out the players who had brought forward the complaints, saying that they had betrayed him. Graham then promised the players that from now on he would put the team first and that they should all just get on with their lives. All of the players but two caved in, and Darren and the other player who stood up to Graham were told to shut up. The team was going to have a hard enough time making the playoffs without all of these problems, so from then on, whatever was said in the dressing room, stayed in the dressing room.

Darren then went to the man who covered the team for the local radio station to tell him what was going on. The team brass found out and that afternoon, Darren was called to the front office and told that he no longer had a position on the team. He was given a cheque for $2,000 and was told to get out of town. Darren also confirmed that the player who charged Graham with me had gone to the team to lodge a complaint but was ignored and that players all over the WHL knew about Graham's activities. Players who had been traded from Swift Current had apparently been telling stories to their teammates and coaches for years about what went on with the Broncos.

It gave me no joy to find out that one of my fears about telling anybody about the abuse had proved legitimate. During my years in Swift Current, I was given many signals from every layer of authority that they did not want to know what Graham was doing with me. I believed that they had wanted me to just keep my mouth shut and score goals. Now I knew I was right. It wouldn't have done any good to tell on Graham.

As more of these allegations and revelations hit the media, I became the human face for sexual abuse survivors everywhere. I was receiving thousands of letters a week from victims, many of them sharing their abuse stories for the first time. Every one of those letters was absolutely heartbreaking. The victims told stories of being molested by the very people they trusted most: teachers, coaches, family members. And all of the victims thanked me for my courage and told me how my example had inspired them to take their own steps toward healing. Jana and I would spend hours reading these letters. The tears in our eyes often made it hard to read.

But in public, I had to play the role of heroic survivor. I had to be a hero but I wasn't even ready to be me. I still felt like a wounded three-year-old child stuck in an adult's body. I was drinking heavily and feeling ashamed of it. When I think of myself at that time, I see a man with a split personality. One of those personalities is a beaten-down drunk drinking out of a paper bag on a street corner. Then the drunk staggers over to a phone booth, gets in, and throws on his Superman cape and goes out to talk to the media. What made me feel even worse was that I had been in treatment for my addictions and hadn't been able to kick them. I felt like I'd run out of excuses. I'd talked about my abuse, put my abuser in jail, received treatment, and inspired thousands of people—why was I still such a mess? No one wanted to talk about that.

The media still wanted a story with a happy ending. They wanted to see the bad guy punished and the good guy rewarded. All of the media profiles ended with Graham behind bars and me talking about how much better I felt. The *Oprah Winfrey Show* was a perfect example. In 1997, Oprah gave some background on the story and interviewed me and Jana. She then introduced Martin Kruze, the Toronto man who blew the whistle on the pedophilia ring that had been run out of Maple Leaf Gardens for decades. Kruze had been abused by at least four Gardens ushers over a seven-year period, and after his story broke in the media, dozens of other victims came forward to press charges. Martin spoke about his own struggles for a little while. The segment closed with a surprise: the wives of the Philadelphia Flyers had raised $50,000 for the Sheldon Kennedy Foundation, a charity that I had recently founded with the help of Tom Laidlaw to help victims of sexual abuse. I was presented with the cheque and the show ended.

Millions of people had watched the *Oprah Winfrey Show* that day. Many of the viewers were sexual abuse victims, and I hoped that my example would encourage them to find help. But what the viewers couldn't see, was the struggle still going on inside me, a struggle that would come close to destroying me over the next eight years, and they couldn't see the struggle that was tearing Martin Kruze apart. A few months later, three days after the man who introduced Martin to the Gardens pedophilia ring was sentenced to two years less a day in jail, Martin committed suicide by throwing himself off the Bloor Street Viaduct in Toronto.

Chapter Six

Things began to die down a little bit as the hockey season came to a close. The Sheldon Kennedy Foundation was up and running and we had a plan for all of the money that we hoped to raise. I came up with the idea of opening a ranch where sexually abused children and their families could go and begin their healing process. The ranch would be staffed by counsellors and experts in child sexual abuse but we would create a family atmosphere. The children would go on nature walks, go fishing, ride dirt bikes and horses—whatever they wanted to do. I wanted the children to forget themselves for a while in the mountains and forests and rivers of the Canadian wild.

I especially wanted the children to be around horses. The company of horses has always made me feel centred and more real somehow. Sometimes it's easier to trust and love an animal than a human being. Most animals are loyal and predictable and respond well to love. The first thing that is taken away from an abused child is their ability to love and trust, so letting them get to know and love a horse would be a stepping stone to learning to love a human being again. The children would also plant trees and be given the task of looking after the saplings. I wanted them to be able to come back to the ranch in five years and see a strong young tree and know that their love and work had nurtured it when it was small and helpless.

Most important, I wanted to take the idea of healing and put it on a level that anyone, even a scared child, could understand. Nothing is scarier for a child than walking into a psychiatrist's office. They have to sit across the desk from somebody who has 8,000 plaques on the wall and are then asked to tell their whole life story, the most painful parts of which have been a secret for so long. Almost anybody would freeze up in an atmosphere like that. I know I had, and I'm a grown man. Children need to feel safe before they can speak about the pain inside them. I wanted to be able to offer kids a very serene setting where they could relax and deal with their issues at their own pace without feeling pressured. The kids would be free to talk when they wanted to talk, and there would be people like me who had been through what they had been through. We would listen to their stories and show them trust and honesty and put them at the centre of the healing process. The children would regain a sense of control over their own lives for the first time since they'd been abused. And when they leave, I wanted them to just hug me and say, "I had a great time and I'd love to come back again."

Then in June, disaster struck my life yet again. I was driving an all-terrain vehicle in rural Alberta along an abandoned railway line. I lost control of the vehicle and it flipped over, pinning my legs underneath. I knew right away that I was badly hurt. The pain nearly made me pass out. As it turned out, my thigh was broken in nine places. I was in shock, stuck under a vehicle in the middle of the bush with no help in sight. I thought I was going to die. My body felt cold from the shock. I just wanted to get out of there. I wanted someone to find me. That was all I could think about. I lay there for two hours before someone came along and found me. I was taken to the hospital, where doctors operated on my shattered thigh, putting the bone back together with pins and plates.

Two days after the surgery, I picked up the paper and saw that the Bruins hadn't picked up the option on my contract. The headline was short and to the point: "Kennedy gets cut." It was news to me. I had no idea I was going to get cut. It took a while for the news to sink in. I was no longer an NHL player. I was twenty years old and unemployed, with a wife and daughter to support and no job prospects in sight. Jana was scared. What were we going to do without my hockey career? I was scared too, but most of all, I felt relief that my hockey career seemed to be over. I didn't want to play hockey anymore. Graham had robbed me of my love of the game fifteen years earlier, and being on an NHL team had begun to feel like having a job where your boss and co-workers spend the whole day punching you in the head.

For the first time in my life, I wanted to make time for me and the people I cared about. I didn't want to be on someone else's schedule. I didn't want to sleep in hotel rooms and eat in restaurants and sit around in airports. It was going to be months before I would be able to walk but I felt truly free for a little while. I would have time to work on my healing and to concentrate on the foundation. I decided that the accident had happened for a reason.

I began doing a number of speaking engagements to drum up interest in the foundation. In August, we had a major fundraising event in Calgary. The Sheldon Kennedy Celebrity Gala began with a golf tournament in the afternoon. Of course, it rained but everyone had a good time and did their best to play in the wet weather. A number of Calgary Flames players were out, along with a number of local celebrities and bigwigs. That night, everyone gathered at the Westin Hotel, where a dinner and silent auction of NHL memorabilia were held. Burton Cummings came out to entertain the crowd.

It was around that time that I met Wayne McNeil, a man who would become one of my best friends and who would do more than just about anybody to make the foundation a success. Wayne was involved with an Albertan microbrewery that was sponsoring a golf tournament to raise funds for the foundation. We met at the tournament and immediately hit it off. He began helping with the foundation, using his business smarts to help us make everything run more efficiently.

The foundation was starting to get off the ground but I knew we had to do more. One day, I was sitting at home and I was watching a documentary about outer space. I thought to myself, "We can spend billions of dollars to send a man to the moon but we can't speak about abuse or do anything to stop it from happening." It blew my mind. There had to be some way to get people talking about this, but how? There was still a lot of media interest in my story, but how could we capitalize on that to raise money? Then in December, I was reading a newspaper and saw that I had been named the Canadian Newsmaker of the Year for 1997 by Canadian Press/Broadcast News. The journalists praised me for charging Graham and opening up dialogue on a topic no one had wanted to even mention. They called what I did a heroic act. They called me brave and said that my courage to speak up forced parents and hockey organizations to question the trust they put in coaches.

After reading the article, the first thing I thought was, "I haven't even done anything." I had charged Graham and identified myself as a victim to save my own life and to try to start my own healing. I knew that my example would help many people who'd been abused and that putting Graham in jail would stop him from hurting any more players but I hadn't actually done anything to help anybody. If I could be named newsmaker of the year without doing anything, imagine what would happen if I really got out there and did something important.

That was when I came up with the idea to in-line skate across Canada to raise money for the ranch and to raise awareness of the cost of sexual abuse in our society. I had only been on in-line skates a few times in my life, and I was still on crutches, but I'd never let facts stand in the way of a plan before. I kept thinking about the skate and then I woke up one night and said to Jana, "I'm going to skate across Canada." She said, "Yeah,

yeah, go back to sleep." But after a couple of more days, it still seemed like a good idea, so I decided I would do it. I had nothing to lose.

When I told Wayne about my idea, he asked me if I'd ever in-line skated in my life. I said, "Not really, but I can learn." I expected him to talk me out of it but he said it sounded like a good idea. As with most important things in life, if you think too much or too long about it, you won't do it. Thank goodness Wayne and I weren't big on thinking, just doing. I asked him if he would volunteer to be president of the foundation and he agreed. We then began restructuring the board over the coming months, adding Lionel Conacher, Dr. Brian Shaw (an expert in child sexual abuse), former Alberta justice minister Brian Evans, and lawyer Gord Kirke.

The dream of opening the ranch got one step closer when a friend of mine, Steven Funk, a Vancouver investment banker, offered to donate a 640-acre parcel of land for the ranch in the interior of British Columbia. I had met Steve and his kids up at my summer place and hit it off with them. When Steve heard about my dream of opening a ranch for abused kids, he decided that he wanted to get involved. The land would be his contribution to the cause. We held a press conference in February to announce our plans to open

Anaphe Ranch in the Kootenay region of the Rocky Mountains. The ranch would be named after Anaphe, the Greek goddess who protects children.

We received a lot of positive media coverage for the press conference. The ranch gave people something more concrete to focus on than just the general issue of preventing child abuse and helping victims of abuse. Anybody could understand the appeal of going back to nature to heal and reflect. A rancher near the proposed site donated a few wild horses that he'd saved from being slaughtered, and the local government unanimously gave their approval to build the ranch.

My doctors told me I was crazy to even think about in-line skating 8,000 kilometres across Canada. My leg needed more time to heal and regain its strength, and there was no saying whether it would ever heal well enough for such a strenuous task. Then there was the question of my mental health. I was still in counselling for my own abuse issues: would I be ready to go out there and talk to the entire nation about what had happened to me? Would I be ready to talk to other abuse victims about their experiences? I was also still abusing alcohol and drugs, and spending months in bed recovering from the accident had left me out of shape.

The board and I began discussing the logistics of putting on an 8,000-kilometre skate. We would need a staff to travel with me to prepare meals, collect donations, set up publicity, speaking engagements, fundraising events, and accommodations, and to help with whatever day-to-day problems arose during the skate. We would need some type of vehicle to carry the staff and give me a place to rest and eat, as well as a central office to co-ordinate everything. Wayne volunteered to take a year off to devote his full-time efforts to help make the skate a reality.

We estimated that building and running the ranch would cost $23 million. We were nowhere near that goal. We needed to start raising more money but we still had a lot of hurdles to jump before we could even get close to our financial targets. Though many people wanted to help out and donate money, we needed to get some of the big corporations behind us. Many of those corporations already had their annual donation budgets committed to established charities like the United Way, arts organizations, children's hospitals, and various cancer research organizations. It's always hard for a new charity to drum up long-term support, and we had the added problem of trying to get companies behind an issue that so many people don't even want to think about. Donating to a charity that was created to eradicate the sexual abuse of children would force the donor to admit that sexual abuse is a big problem in our society, and I was quickly finding out that many people had trouble accepting this reality or even talking about it.

There was also the issue of my own checkered past. My past behaviour made people a little wary of supporting a cause with my name attached to it in spite of the goodwill I had inspired by coming forward and charging Graham. Some people who wanted to support the cause decided to take a wait-and-see stance. If we couldn't get them to donate any actual money, there were plenty of goods and services that we would need for the four-month skate. I began speaking to many corporate boards about the skate and the ranch. I turned a lot of heads when I hobbled into the boardroom on a pair of crutches promising everybody that in six months I'd be ready to in-line skate from Newfoundland to British Columbia.

Eventually, some of the big organizations got behind us. Nike, Molson, The Co-operators insurance company, the Calgary Flames, and other companies donated some money and many useful goods and services to help the skate. Imperial Oil gave us free gas for the entire skate. We secured a very reasonable lease rate on a massive RV and hired a group of dedicated students to work for the duration of the skate. We also decided to hire Don Smith, a therapist who specialized in sexual abuse, to accompany us to help anyone who wanted to talk about their abuse experiences.

It took months of preparation and fundraising but by May, we were ready to roll. On May 30, 1998, I strapped on my blades in St. John's, dipped my feet in the Atlantic, and set off for Vancouver Island on the other side of Canada. We had millions of dollars to raise and we still needed more corporate funding but we hoped as the skate gained momentum, more companies would get on board. We were determined to achieve our goals and we would figure out how to do it along the way if that's what it took. I'd also had a lot of time to think about the ranch, and I was starting to see that educating the public about the dangers of sexual abuse was at least as important as giving the victims of abuse a place to heal. I was still getting thousands of letters from childhood sexual-abuse victims, many of them in their fifties, sixties, and seventies, thanking me for going public with my abuse issues. Some of them had never told anybody about their abuse and many had only recently come out as survivors because of my example. We had to get people to

Mile Zero: Me and Wayne McNeil in St. John's, Newfoundland, on the first day of the skate. We had no idea what we were getting ourselves into.

start speaking openly about abuse or the terrible suffering would keep passing from one generation to the next. I said to Jana the day before I left for St. John's that if I didn't raise a dime but touched the life of at least one person, the whole thing will have been worth it for me.

There were still questions about whether I was in good enough shape to do the skate. I hadn't done as much training as I should have but I knew I could do it. Wayne wasn't so sure. I kept saying to him, "Wayner, I've skated all my life," but he kept on my case about it. Finally, about a week before the skate started, I told Wayne to grab his bike. We went to Fish Creek Park in Calgary and I wheeled off a quick 60 kilometres in the pouring rain, as much to piss him off as to prove I could do it. By the end, we were both soaked and frozen. He never asked again about my in-line skating abilities.

We set up two teams for the skate. The first was the Skate Team, consisting of me and five brave university students: Gord Ross, Shawna Campbell, Chantelle Vooys, Cindy Willick, and Sheldon Romashenko. They assisted with the tour in every imaginable way on the road, every day, all day, for the entire skate. They were amazing. They were able to manage what Wayne called the equivalent of planning and running a large wedding every day, back to back, for nearly five months. For them, the skate was a physical and emotional roller coaster but they never wavered, bickered, or strayed from the cause.

The Base Team consisted of Wayne, Marj Perry (our administrative leader), Jana, and Rosemary Wilson. They focused on trying to keep the overall logistics intact and running a professional charitable organization. They worked with communities prior to the Skate Team's arrival to set up special events and also handled fundraising and corporate sponsorships. Wayne was also dealing with the media on a day-to-day basis. Throughout the skate, we had several other part-time staff and volunteers who assisted on several fronts. Our offices in Calgary were a continuous hub of energy for almost a year.

That first day in St. John's began very early in the morning with a trip to the grounds of Mount Cashel, an orphanage that had been run by the Christian Brothers, a Roman Catholic religious order. The institute made international headlines in the 1980s when dozens of former students charged the Brothers with hundreds of counts of physical and sexual abuse spanning a fifty-year period. Many of the Brothers were convicted of multiple counts of abuse, though few of them served more than two years in jail. Jana and I went to the site with one of the victims, now a grown man and still haunted by his memories of the institution. I hung a wreath on the site and hoped the gesture would help the surviving victims turn a page in their lives.

We had a meeting at 8:00 a.m. in St. John's with

Jana and Ryan get ready for another day on the road.

our crew. We went over the day's schedule and tried to prepare ourselves for the crazy mission we were about to undertake. We had 8,000 kilometres and four months of road ahead of us. We were nervous but excited. Everybody knew what their jobs were. We had phone numbers for local distress lines and contact names for counselling centres in the area in case anyone we met along the way disclosed their own sexual abuse story and needed help. I would be doing a short skate that day and then all of us would take a short plane ride to Sydney, Nova Scotia, where the RV and the rest of our crew were waiting for us.

Jana and I and a couple of the crew met at the town hall and from there I skated into the downtown core, accompanied by a number of policemen on in-line skates. Hundreds of people turned out at the harbour to wish us luck. I gave a short speech and dipped my skates in the Atlantic. Our crew had set up a large canvas and asked the local children to dip their hands in paint and press their palms onto the canvas, which would one day hang at the ranch. From there, I skated through town and southwards for a few hours. We collected over $4,000 that first day, pretty good considering that it rained that afternoon. At first I was afraid that I was going to get run down by some pedophile who'd just gotten out of jail. I had no idea what to expect. Many people hadn't heard of the skate, so our staff spent a lot of time going into communities that we would be passing through and bringing people up to speed on what we were doing. When folks heard what the money was for, they gladly threw cash into the donation bags. The government enquiry into the Mount Cashel abuse scandal was still fresh in everybody's minds, so people were pretty responsive to our cause. We also got a lot of media coverage that day. All in all, it was a good start to the trip.

The skate picked up the next morning in Syndey. Sydney is on Cape Breton Island, the easternmost part of Nova Scotia. I didn't know much about the area but I soon became very acquainted with the island's hills and low mountains, especially Kelly's Mountain, a slow seven-kilometre climb that I thought was going to kill me. My body was not used to the strain and I hadn't quite figured out a proper food regimen. I was going on pure adrenaline, wearing out a set of roller wheels every day. I would have to ice my leg muscles every day to prevent too much lactic acid buildup. My body slowly adjusted to the gruelling schedule but I was exhausted most of the time. We were all learning as we went. There were hundreds of logistical details that we hadn't expected—just making sure the crew was properly fed and accommodated every day and night was a major undertaking. At one town in Nova Scotia, no one seemed to know we were coming. Only one person came out to meet us but he and I had a great conversation. There were many frustrating hours for all of us but our team never let the setbacks and exhaustion get them down. They got me out of bed every morning when I was exhausted and sore and afraid of facing crowds of strangers. They were always there for me.

As news of the skate spread across Canada, increasingly larger crowds turned out to cheer us on. People parked their cars in the ditches at the side of the highway and stood on the shoulders and applauded and called out to me. We were doing 100 kilometres and up to five speaking engagements a day. I spoke at churches, town halls, arenas, parking lots, parks, town squares, bingo halls. Everywhere I looked, I saw crowds of people and cameras and tape recorders. People hugged me, kissed me, shook my hand, and patted me on the back. They invited me into their homes and we invited them into the RV. They honked and waved from their cars and bikes and motorcycles and trucks. The best of all were the children who turned out to skate and bike with me for a while. Being around children always makes me feel better. They give me what I need: trust, enthusiasm, laughter, and love. One journalist, seeing me skating into town with dozens of children, described me as a pied piper. That sounded just about right. I was the pied piper trying to lead these children toward knowledge that could protect them from ever being victims. As a kid, I'd never heard of child abuse. When it happened to me, I just knew that it didn't feel good, but I didn't know how to explain it to anyone.

People didn't always know how to react when they saw me. When Terry Fox ran into town, people could see the damage that cancer had done to his body. But I was in great shape and had long curly locks and a smiling face, so a lot of people wondered, *Where is the damage?* He's healthy. He played for almost ten years in the NHL. The very fact that people couldn't see the damage was what made the skate so powerful and opened so many minds to the damage of sexual abuse. You can't see a bruise on the brain and on the heart, so it's hard for people to understand the damage that abuse does to victims. The more I thought about this, the more I realized that the focal point of the skate had to be to educate people about the real suffering of abuse victims. The point of the skate was to make visible something invisible.

Most people I met along the way were glad to support a cause that had been in the closet for so long. Everyone knows that sexual abuse happens

One of the quiet moments early in the skate.

but they don't know how to begin to talk about the problem. It's hard enough for most people to talk about sex between consenting adults in public, but when you bring in sex between adults and children, well, people don't want to even think about that, never mind talk about it. And who can blame them? The sexual abuse of children is a violation of everything our society holds sacred but people have to start talking about it or it will never stop. The skate was giving people a chance to finally start a dialogue around the issue. I was giving them a face and a story to help start that dialogue but they also needed to realize that whether they were aware of it or not, someone they loved was a sexual abuse survivor. Most experts agree that one out of every four women and one of out every six men will be sexually abused by the age of eighteen; though as time goes on and more victims disclose their abuse, those estimates are creeping closer to one in three women and one in four men. My own experience and the experience of many police officers, counsellors, and doctors I've spoken to puts that figure even higher.

Although many people had trouble understanding the amount of sexual abuse that happens at every level of our society, the victims I met along the way certainly didn't. During the skate, ten to fifteen people a day would disclose their abuse stories to me. I was often the first person they had told. A lot of them were adults, men and women who were twenty years old and older who'd experienced abuse as children. At one stop, a seventy-year-old man came up to me with tears streaming down his face and told me his story and thanked me. Every one of those stories was heartbreaking, and every story was basically the same. The details varied but every victim was betrayed by an adult they trusted and then felt so ashamed and guilty that they kept silent about the abuse. The emotional cost of this silence and shame was always the same: addictions, wasted potential, loss of relationships, loss of intimacy, suicide attempts, mental illness—an endless river of suffering.

Seeing me out there talking about these issues seemed to give the survivors hope. They knew that they were not alone. They could see me on a podium talking about my abuse and would think to themselves, "It's not just me! I'm not crazy. I'm not a freak. And maybe, just maybe, the abuse wasn't my fault." A policeman in Ontario told me that he used my story to help a fourteen-year-old boy come forward to press charges against his abuser. I met a man who told me that he had charged a former teacher with sexual abuse after I charged Graham and told my story in the media. These are just two of the thousands of stories I heard. I listened to every one of them, no matter how long it took, and I told the survivor my story when I thought it would help. But I'm not a psychologist. I didn't really know how to help them. I could only listen and try to be there for them and advise them to get help. I was still so far away from truly dealing with my own abuse issues but I couldn't tell that to the thousands of people I met along the way. So I did what I always did: I drank, I did drugs, I ran from my emotions. I was determined to make the skate a success and help everyone I could along the way but I still had no idea how to help myself.

I knew the skate was getting bigger than anyone of us could have imagined when Wayne and I were invited to have breakfast with the prime minister on Canada Day. I couldn't believe that! The only problem was that we were running late before we even left the hotel, all the streets were blocked off, and I had nothing dressy to wear. We were in a frenzy. I begged the people at the hotel to lend me a suit and Wayne pleaded with an RCMP officer to give us an escort. We rang the bell at the Prime Minister's official residence and Jean Chrétien himself opened the door. He was still buttoning his shirt, which made us feel at ease. I was so at ease that I apologized for my shin-high pants by telling him that I felt like Jethro Clampett from *The Beverly Hillbillies*. I'm sure the Prime Minister had no idea who Jethro was but he chuckled anyway. As I looked around the beautiful house, I said, "Nice digs," to which he replied, "Not bad for subsidized housing." We were all on the same wavelength that day. Mr. Chrétien was a great guy, very down to earth. He thanked me for the work I was doing for the country, but mostly we just talked about hockey and joked around with each other. Later, I took part in the Canada Day festivities and visited a homeless shelter for men.

A few days later, we skated into Toronto. We headed for the downtown core from the east and

Canada Day, 1998: Wayne and I share a laugh with Prime Minister Jean Chrétien at his official residence in Ottawa.

were accompanied by police cruisers and officers on bikes and dozens of cars and trucks. There were hundreds of cyclists and in-line skaters weaving in and out of the skate to cheer me on. When we came to the Bloor Street Viaduct, I stopped for a while. This was where Martin Kruze had committed suicide after learning that his chief abuser would only have to serve two years in prison for abusing God only knows how many young men. As I looked down at the Don Valley Parkway far below, I thought about how much Martin would have

Another day, another speech.

enjoyed this day. It might have made him feel a little better to see how many people were getting out to support the cause. At the same time, I could understand why he had killed himself that day. I can remember many occasions where I felt so low that the only thing that made me feel better was the thought of suicide, of escaping from my own skin and leaving this world.

We headed down to Carlton Street, where hundreds of well-wishers and reporters waited for us at Maple Leaf Gardens. Many past and present Maple Leafs were there, including Mats Sundin, Tie Domi, and Glen Healey, as well as team president and ex-Canadiens goalie Ken Dryden and Cassie Campbell

Accepting one of the hundreds of oversized cheques donated to the skate, this one from Tom Davies representing the good folks at the Sudbury Regional Police Association/Fitness Committee.

from the Canadian national women's hockey team. The Leafs presented us with a cheque for $20,000 and a number of the players joined me as I skated to the Skydome, where I threw the ceremonial first pitch. The Blue Jays provided me and the crew with a catered luxury box. Later, Mayor Mel Lastman gave me the key to Toronto, and all I could say was, "Awesome."

The skate chugged north from Toronto. I was presented with cheques and citations and flowers and gifts from community leaders, children, mayors, councillors, native elders, premiers, and businessmen, but most of the money came from individuals who dropped loonies and toonies into our collection buckets. We stopped for a while at the Terry Fox memorial outside of Thunder Bay. The statue was built near the spot where Terry's Marathon of Hope came to an early end on September 1, 1980. The cancer that cost him his right leg had spread to his lungs and he was forced to fly home, where he died less than a year later.

In August, my mother joined the skate for two weeks at the Ontario/Manitoba border. I was physically exhausted and emotionally drained but my mother could see that I was happier than I had been in a long time. She saw that I could talk to people and look them in the eyes and not be afraid. She heard me laughing again and kidding around with people. Seeing me like that made her feel better. She had suffered so much after learning what Graham had done to me for all those years. She felt guilty and blamed herself for not protecting me. This is one of the many hidden costs of sexual abuse: the guilt and self-hatred that family members feel when they find out that they could not protect a child from abuse. The parents blame themselves for not reading the signs, for leaving their children with the very person who abused them.

Home again: hoisting the Manitoba flag after the long trek through Ontario.

It broke my heart to see my mother blaming herself for not protecting me from Graham but I tried to tell her that it wasn't her fault. I explained to her that Graham had fooled everybody, that he was a master manipulator, a serial predator who preyed on the decency and trust of the parents and communities whose children he had sworn to protect. She told me that she had been taught to prepare one's daughters, to look out for the bad guys who would try to rape them. She hadn't thought that there were people out there who did that to boys. I told her that's what the skate was all about: educating people about every form of childhood abuse so that they could better protect their children.

I hooked up with many of my relatives and old friends as we made our way across the Prairies. My brother joined us near Brandon and he biked into our hometown of Elkhorn with a bunch of our cousins and friends. The folks in Elkhorn gave me a hero's welcome and donated thousands of dollars to the cause. We unveiled a new sign at the entrance to town that read "Welcome to Elkhorn: The Proud Home of Sheldon Kennedy," and that night, a banquet was held in my honour. My mom, Troy, Jana, Ryan, and I got to spend time with old family friends and guys I'd played hockey with. It felt good to come into town without feeling ashamed of how I hadn't lived up to my potential

Greeting the well-wishers outside the Manitoba legislature in Winnipeg. It was crowds like this that kept me going most days.

and how I kept screwing up my life.

We continued across the Prairies and made it into Alberta by the end of August. In Edmonton, I had dinner with the premier, who gave $15,000 to the foundation. My friend Darcy arranged for me to use a brand new Hummer. I wrote in my journal: "Got rid of the minivan today to make way for our Hummer! Humma Humma Humma! Can't wait to take that bad boy for a spin!" I took it for a spin all right. After drinking about eight beers I crashed the Hummer into a guardrail. The vehicle sustained about $20,000 worth of damage. A friend of mine was with in the Hummer but neither of us was hurt. It was an idiotic thing to do. I don't know

My triumphant return to Swift Current, Saskatchewan.

what I was thinking. Nothing, I suppose. I just wanted to forget myself for a while, be an ordinary guy driving a big car, not a national hero carrying the hopes of millions of sexual abuse victims on his shoulders. I was fined by the police for leaving the accident scene.

The next day, I couldn't believe what I'd done, but the accident showed me that I still had so much more healing to do. There were times where I'd start thinking, "I'm through this, I'm better now." But the Hummer incident was like someone knocking at my back door. I answered the door and there were all my old problems just saying, "Hello, Sheldon, we're still here. Don't forget about us!" It was a slap in the face.

My grandmother met me in Red Deer and

Innisfail, where my father was living. My dad and I spent a little time together. Like my mother, he felt terrible guilt for not protecting me from Graham. He was interviewed by *Western Report* magazine and talked about the changes that came over me after I met Graham. He told them how I found it hard to even be in the same room with him anymore. "It almost seemed like Sheldon was trying to keep an action between us," he said. "Something was always more important than being alone with me. Even when he was standing still, he'd be pacing. Looking back, it makes sense. If you're not alone, no one can ask questions." About Graham, he said: "He came into our home pretending to be a friend, but all the time he was manipulating all of us. I should have checked things out. As a parent, you can't leave anything unchecked." I hoped that every parent in the country would read what my father said that day.

Wayne was able to join us at a very moving event held at the Morley Native Reserve just outside of Calgary. As I skated north off the Trans-Canada Highway toward the reserve, the road swelled with people and pickup trucks to escort me. I stopped at the community centre, where, in a large circle, they welcomed me, made me an honorary brother, conducted a traditional ceremony, and shared sweet grass. I gave a talk in the audito-

How many more miles?

The crew takes a breather in Banff, Alberta.

rium and felt immediately connected with everyone in there. The native communities I visited
across the country were incredibly supportive.
Even with all the damage done to them in residen-
tial schools, they treated me with compassion and
respect. There wasn't a dry eye in the place that
night. When we went back to the mobile home, we
were all balling. "It's like this all the time," the
Skate Team explained to Wayne. He was in tears
and could only mutter, "Unbelievable, this is what
it's all about."

When I was just beginning to experience the
crazy climbs of the Canadian Rockies, the story
about the Hummer crash, and the fact that I had
left the accident scene, was all over the media. We

Me, Jana, and Ryan on the ferry to Vancouver Island, our last stop on the five-month journey.

decided that the best thing to do was hold a press conference back in Calgary. I faced the cameras and reporters and just tried to speak from my heart. I told them that I was deeply disappointed in my actions in Edmonton and that I apologize to my family, my friends, my foundation, and the thousands of supporters of my foundation. I tried to explain that the incident was a relapse and that I wasn't as far on my own healing journey as I would have liked. I said that I was only beginning to realize that it would take a lifetime to get over the damage. "I feel guilty," I said. "I feel I've let everybody down. I hope they can understand the damage I've done. I'm seen as a role model and a hero. I've never been comfortable with that. I only wanted to help as many people as I could. I got so focused on trying to help others that I forgot to help myself. I've never said I'm anything more than an abuse victim who's trying to make a difference. The thing now is to get back to the skate and finish it."

That was one of the worst days of my life. One sympathetic journalist, Peter Stockland from *The Calgary Herald*, wrote that my eyes were "a dead giveaway of the pain that abuse victims can never completely control… The tears, when they came, seemed not only heartfelt but soul-torn." That just about summed it up. Other journalists praised me for being so frank about what I'd done and reminded readers that the damage of sexual abuse does not disappear overnight. Other writers were not as sympathetic. I was accused of wallowing in self-pity, of making excuses for my behaviour, and of being a big disappointment to all the people who looked up to me. I was told to get on with my life. If only it were that easy. Wayne admitted to the media that therapists who had counselled me in the past had called to ask if I was okay being out on the road and in front of all those people and cameras. They wondered how I was able to carry the torch for other abuse victims when I obviously wasn't dealing with my own problems. But we only had one more province to skate through. I was physically and emotionally exhausted. We could think about my abuse issues later.

The last leg of the skate took me through the mountains of British Columbia and some of the toughest days of the marathon. It felt like I was skating uphill the whole way, up and down mountains and hills. I just wanted to finish the skate and get home at that point. Everywhere I went, reporters asked me about the Hummer incident. I couldn't say sorry enough times about what I'd done. But my family and team and the people I met along the way kept me going.

I visited the Mission Institute, a federal prison in Abbotsford. When you think of a maximum security prison, you think of chains and slamming doors and hardened criminals, but I quickly calmed down as I walked into the prison chapel and was greeted by applause, handshakes, and hugs from about forty inmates. I addressed the prisoners, telling them about my own story and what I hoped to accomplish with the skate. I told the men that the issue could not be overlooked any more and that sweeping it under the carpet only prolonged the pain. The effect on the inmates was incredible. Grown men with tattooed arms wept as they told their tales of child abuse. Every man in that room had a story to tell about sexual abuse that they had suffered. Some were even in jail for murdering their abusers. Again and again I heard the same stories that every victim I met on the road shared with me, stories of addiction, self-abuse, broken families, descent into a life of crime, and the victimizing of innocent people. Native inmate Tom Elder presented me with an eagle feather, saying it represented truth and honour. He told me that the eagle flies high and flies alone, and that the eagle feather is one of the highest honours you could give someone.

On October 11th, the skate finally came to an end with a ceremony and a dip in the Pacific with my mom. After four months and 8,000 kilometres and got the whole country talking about the horrors of sexual abuse. Hundreds of people and local dignitaries were there to congratulate me. I told everyone that I was really proud of the way the people of Canada had reacted, and that after this weekend, we would sit down and start to finalize the plans for the ranch and start turning the dream into a reality. There were a lot of tears that day. I felt good but completely drained. I had accomplished what I'd set out to do. Now I just wanted to go home and spend some time with my wife and daughter.

Chapter Seven

It's hard to explain how things went so wrong for me in the years following the skate. I had felt good for much of the cross-country tour. Preparing for and completing the skate had put me in the zone for a while. I had had a mission. I was focused. Every day brought me challenges that I could see in front of me and then try to accomplish. I could see that what we were doing was touching the lives of hundreds of thousands of people, and that made me feel good, even if hearing so many stories of abuse left me feeling drained and depressed at times. It felt nice to give something back to the world and it felt good to do something that I could feel proud of. The skate helped keep the topic of sexual abuse in the papers long enough and often enough for the average person to talk about the problem over their morning coffee. After they talked about it for a while, many people were able to start helping loved ones who were struggling with abuse issues. In many cases, this dialogue around abuse helped them to admit that they too were victims. Victims and their loved ones were allowed to feel less ashamed about their abuse and less alone in their struggles.

The media really helped us get this dialogue going, and I will always be grateful to them. They brought abuse into the spotlight so that every Canadian with a TV, radio, or newspaper subscription had to think about the issue, at least for a few minutes. But too often the media turned my life story into a kind of fairy tale. The hero Sheldon Kennedy survives abuse, puts his abuser in jail, cries on TV a few times, and feels better, then skates across Canada to raise money for other victims. It wasn't like that. I wasn't a hero. I was still in pain and still miles away from anything near a recovery. I could never explain how deep the scars went, in me and everyone else who's ever been molested. I wanted every reporter who interviewed me to pick up a book on the long-term effects of abuse and read it and explain these realities to the general public. I wanted to see articles and news segments on the broader issues of sexual abuse—the number of victims, how and why the abuse was allowed to continue, why so few victims reported their abuse to the authorities, but almost every journalist I met asked me the same questions: What's it like on the road? What are you going to do next? Can you tell us about the ranch? I know the reporters were just doing their job the best they could and that they had plenty of other stories to work on, but their questions just seemed to gloss over the very issue that I wanted everyone to understand. I felt as if I could have had five articles written at the beginning of the skate and reprinted them over and over again.

Being hailed as a hero by the media and so many people I met along the way made me feel like I had pulled the wool over everybody's eyes, just as I'd pulled the wool over everyone's eyes since I met Graham. Being Sheldon the Hero was just another role I was playing, a way of hiding from the real person inside me. Even with all the therapy and disclosure, I still felt like I hadn't dealt with the emotional pain. The physical part of the abuse is not what lingers. The physical abuse was like having an arm broken: the limb hurts but the bones heal and you move on, scarred but whole. It's the shame that never goes away, the feeling of loneliness, and then the shame of being a drunk, which makes for double shame. After the skate ended, I went back to my old life and my old destructive patterns. I was completely exhausted, physically and emotionally, and I had no plans for the future. I was still anxious, ashamed, and having trouble sleeping. To make myself feel better, I drank and smoked pot. The same old story.

In October 1998, I decided to travel to Stony Mountain, Manitoba for Graham's parole hearing.

I didn't know what to expect. Part of me wanted to find some kind of closure. I wanted to know if Graham finally understood that he done something terribly wrong to me and all of his other victims. I knew in my heart that he would be the same old Graham but I needed to see for myself. My mother came with me to the hearing. I just sat in the courtroom and stared at Graham's back. He was thinner and had more grey hair than the last time I'd seen him in court. He stood up and told a two-man parole panel his version of how he had molested me and two other players while he was our hockey coach.

"I am sure the effect has been horrific, ranging from confusion to anger to shame," Graham said. "I had no thought of the consequences and ramifications. It was an outlet for desire – the need to be close with someone, to be closer to someone than a coach should be. I convinced myself this was a physical act – no big deal. I did not get into hockey to get into young men. I became a coach before I was aware where my sexual persuasion would take me. If I wanted to continue in hockey, I could see no other way but to conceal who I was. I abused that advice parents gave to their sons: "Listen to your coach." I betrayed the trust, confidence, and faith they had in me. I've betrayed my conscience. At last I am wide awake."

The judge obviously believed Graham. He said that Graham was "likely to be a candidate for successful reintroduction into the community," then sentenced him to a concurrent six months of day parole. Graham was now a free man. Graham the serial molester would now be walking the streets again. I'd met guys who'd gotten longer sentences for dealing drugs or stealing cars, and here was a man who'd admitted to more than 350 counts of sexual abuse against a minor walking free after serving less than two years in jail. All he had to do was stand up there and say he was sorry. He had taken the stand and painted a beautiful picture with words, just as he always did when he wanted to cover up his true intentions and feelings. And he was still using the same excuse he'd used when he was sexually abusing me: that he was a homosexual who could not come out publicly because he worked in the macho world of pro hockey. But this was not a case of being gay. Gay men do not have sex with boys any more than straight men have sex with little girls. To equate pedophilia and homosexuality is insulting to gay people everywhere but that's what Graham continued to do. Graham never used the word *pedophile* to describe his sexual orientation. He never really admitted that what he had done was a crime that destroyed the lives of his victims. He didn't talk about his sick need to control every aspect of his victim's lives. He didn't admit he was a stalker, a manipulator, and that he used threats to get what he wanted. Worst of all, he didn't come clean about all of the other boys he molested. This was not a man who wanted healing and repentance. This was a man who wanted out of jail so that he could get back on with his life.

I was interviewed by reporters after the hearing. I told them that it hadn't bothered me to see Graham again. As for whether I thought Graham was cured, I pointed out that I had been receiving professional help for a lot longer than he had and that I was still a long way from healing. I told them that no one can be cured of pedophilia in two years, especially when they couldn't even admit that they were a pedophile. I told them that I saw the same Graham James up there on the stand who had molested me all those years ago. My mother just said, "Let's hope he gets healed."

Now that the skate had ended, we had to figure how much money we had raised and what we should do with it. We were nowhere near the $23-million mark and we had no real plans for raising substantial amounts of money to build the ranch. On top of that, the biggest issue with the ranch wasn't the land or the building but rather the ongoing costs. We would have to make a huge commitment to raising operating funds year in and year out. With horses, outdoor activities, and young people needing supervision, the cost of maintaining and insuring the ranch would be astronomical. One of our plans was to set up a trial program at a ranch outside of Calgary.

Wayne began doing some research on the challenges facing the foundation. Most organizations that Wayne spoke to that treated abused kids liked the idea of their patients "getting away" but were not eager to have their patients change caregivers during treatment. They wanted a place to go but not necessarily the infrastructure we had envisioned. Wayne also discovered that there were many treatment environments across Canada already in place, but very few prevention programs. Everything we had learned on the skate told us that the foundation's priority should be the prevention of sexual abuse of children. Wayne set out to find the best prevention program in Canada, with the possible aim of donating all of our funds to them. We were considering closing the book on the Sheldon Kennedy Foundation, and we wanted all the the monies we'd raised going to the organization that could do the most to prevent abuse.

Then in December, the media decided to focus

its attention on the fact that I had taken a $7,500 monthly salary during the five months of the skate. Reporters and columnists accused me of being greedy, of misrepresenting the foundation, and even insinuated that I did the skate just to put money in my own pocket. Almost everyone in the media agreed that I should never have taken a cent for the skate. It hurt me to read this, but it hurt even more to read the reactions of many people who had donated money to the foundation wrote to the newspapers saying that I had betrayed them. I tried to explain to the media that it was the board's decision to pay me for the skate and that the money I received was also meant to cover the year of full-time work I had put into the foundation leading up to the skate, for which I had not received a penny. This meant that the entire time that I worked full-time raising money for the foundation—five months of which involved working 16-hour days, seven days a week—I drew an annual salary of about $37,500. But the papers just kept flashing the same headline: Sheldon Kennedy received $7,500 a month to skate across Canada.

The truth was that after finishing in the NHL, I was basically broke. I had blown money like there was no tomorrow when I played hockey. To make myself feel better for a few moments, I would go and buy things: drugs, cars, boats, clothes. Jana helped me get the spending under control, but by then, I had blown most of the money I made in my first five years in the NHL. I still had a mortgage to pay and a child to support and no other way of earning an income. Five months without a paycheque was not an option for me anymore. Jana also worked in the Calgary office all that summer without drawing a paycheque. How were we supposed to eat? I tried to be straightforward about this salary, pointing out that, unlike many other charity events, ours was not sponsored by any corporations. There was no one to pay our expenses but ourselves and the money we raised on the skate. I was slated to receive a modest salary for the rest of the year, but after I signed with the Manitoba Moose of the AHL in October, I told the board that I wouldn't be needing any more money. These arguments didn't stop many journalists from casting a negative light on the foundation and the skate. Other members of the media reported very fairly on the story but the damage was already done. It was going to be even harder to raise money for the foundation if we chose to stick with it.

In the months following the skate, the foundation was raised in discussions with the Canadian Red Cross Abuse Prevention Services, an organization that runs the largest and most successful national abuse-prevention program in Canada, reaching 65,000 children, volunteers, and community leaders each year. Wayne had met the Red Cross supporters when we concluded the skate in Vancouver and was intrigued by their programs. We decided that my goal of educating all Canadians on the issue of child abuse would best be served by joining forces with the Red Cross. In June of 1999, the foundation announced that all of its assets, in excess of $1 million dollars, would be transferred to the Canadian Red Cross Abuse Prevention Services (APS). I accepted a full-time position with APS in its public affairs department. In this role, I could continue to be an important spokesperson in the crusade against child abuse by travelling across Canada speaking to numerous school groups, parents, and sports organizations.

There was still so much prevention and education work to do, and there still is. This was really brought home to me in May 2000 when Mike Brophy wrote a full-page feature piece on Graham for *The Hockey News*. Graham had been banned from coaching for life by the International Ice Hockey Federation, but in the article, Brophy argued that Graham should be given the opportunity to coach youth hockey. He said that Graham "did his time" and that he "should come with a loud warning label so everyone who comes in contact with him is aware of his past." A warning label? That makes about as much sense as putting a warning label on a car driven by a drunk driver—that label isn't going to help anyone unlucky enough to get in the way of the car. Brophy was just reflecting the attitude that allowed Graham to get away with what he did for so long, that if a coach gets results on the ice, we'll just ignore what he does off the ice. We'll just overlook the fact that he's a repeat sexual offender who has preyed on the very age group and gender that he'd be coaching.

This represents total ignorance of pedophilia. Pedophilia is not a lifestyle choice, it is a nearly incurable illness. Police estimate that most pedophiles will abuse 70 children before they are turned in by one of the victims. Studies also show that approximately one out of four male victims will eventually go on to sexually abuse children. Do the math. And then consider that Graham is now coaching hockey for the Spanish national team. Why a man with his extensive criminal record was allowed out of the country after serving his parole time is another matter. It's a good thing he wasn't a convicted drug dealer, or he probably wouldn't have been allowed to leave.

There is also the recent case of Mike Danton, a former NHL player with the St. Louis Blues, who is now in prison after being convicted of planning the murder of his former junior-hockey coach and agent, David Frost. When Danton was eleven, his father introduced him to Frost, thinking the coach could improve Danton's chances of making the NHL. Frost got the results on the ice and Danton's career picked up. When he was sixteen, Danton and three other players lived with Frost in a hotel room in Deseronto, Ontario, where they played for a team called the Quinte Hawks.

Seven years later, Frost became the target of Danton's murder-for-hire plot. Frost became Danton's mentor, coach, and agent, and Danton followed his hockey and life instructions in a way other coaches have described as cultlike. The head of the Greater Toronto Hockey League (GTHL), where Frost coached Danton, told the CBC that Frost "practiced mind control" ("In Depth: The Mike Danton Case," *CBC Sports Online*, Nov. 30, 2005). If people thought something funny was going on, why didn't they do something about it? And why was a grown man allowed to live with four minors in a hotel room? Why didn't social workers or league officials talk to these boys and find out what was going on? Why did everyone trust Frost with these young people's lives? Danton's father says he overlooked the strangeness of his son's relationship with Frost because the results were showing up on the ice and the thought of having a son in the NHL was too enticing.

There are still too many parents willing to turn their children over to near strangers because they think it will help their kids get a better shot at the NHL. The same is true in other sports, this in spite of the fact that a survey done in the mid-1990s concluded that 22% of Olympic athletes in Canada had sexual intercourse with an authority figure in their lives, usually their coach. Of those surveyed, 80% said that they were aware of some form of sexual abuse, harassment, or assault of their fellow athletes. You only have to think of the hundreds of recent charges laid against priests, teachers, coaches, and prison guards to realize that children need to be protected at all times. We can never take their safety for granted. They have to know that they can talk about anything with their parents and that when bad things happen to them it is not their fault.

It didn't take long for my addiction problems to get to a very bad point again. My stint in the AHL did not work out and I left after just over 20 games. I played for a team in Germany for 10 games but I just couldn't get back into the rhythm. I was exhausted for at least two years after the skate and had no idea what to do with myself. My drinking and drug use got so bad that I had trouble keeping up my responsibilities with the Red Cross. Eventually, in 1998, with the help of Dr. Brian Shaw and the NHLPA, I entered a treatment program in California, where I spent nine months confronting my abuse issues.

The treatment centre was great for me while I was there. The intensive therapy program forced me to really go deep into the pain that I carried with me day in, day out. One of the things I came to realize was how much pain I had been inflicting on Jana. I hadn't done this on purpose but I had done it all the same. I was so grateful for everything that she had done for me that I couldn't bear the thought of dragging her through the mud anymore. After a few months of therapy at the centre, I decided to get a divorce. I wanted her to be free of my suffering and start to live a little more for herself. I wanted her to be happy again, and she would never be able to do that while she was married to me. It was the most difficult decision I ever had to make but I was glad I did it.

I also used my time at the centre to enter a serious physical training program for the first time. I worked with a trainer every day at a local Gold's Gym and soon I was in the best physical shape of my life. I even began to think about trying to return to the NHL when I got out of treatment. But then one day, I herniated myself while working out. It would take months to recover from the injury. I wasn't quite ready to admit it to myself, but my hockey career was over.

I left the treatment centre feeling confident that I was on the road to recovery. I was probably too confident. I did have a much better understanding of the pain and shame that were lodged deep inside me, but like a lot of people trying to recover from abuse and addiction, I believed that once I confronted the problem, I would become a new man. I thought that I just needed to get off the booze and drugs and talk about my abuse and then all the shame and guilt would be lifted off of my shoulders like an old suit of armour that I didn't need anymore. Maybe it's necessary to believe this, because if you knew just how long and hard the recovery process is, you might never even begin. I had to fall a few times before I realized that healing was going to be a lifelong journey.

I returned to Calgary in June 2000 and got a place on my own downtown. I had no idea what I wanted to do with my life. All I had ever done was play hockey and be a spokesperson for sexual abuse survivors. Neither of those jobs appealed to me. I was doing some consulting work with Hockey Canada but that only took up about four weekends a year. I began to realize that, in spite of all the work I'd done at the treatment centre, I still did not know how to live on a day-to-day basis. I didn't know how to look after myself. I didn't know how to let off steam or get help when life got me down. In the past, whenever something bothered me, I drank or smoked a joint. That was how I coped and got through the day. Now that I had taken those crutches away, I had no idea what to replace them with.

The only thing that kept me going were the days that I spent with Ryan. She gave me hope that I could become a better man, but how to become that better man was a problem I was having trouble solving. My life was going nowhere. I felt depressed and anxious. But now I had no more excuses. I had gotten to the bottom of my pain: why couldn't I move on with my life? I still believed that all the therapy I had gone through had made me strong enough to handle using alcohol and drugs again, so I started getting drunk occasionally and smoking a joint or two. Soon, I started skipping the meetings that were part of the treatment centre's recovery program. I told myself didn't need them. I just needed to find something to do and get on with my life.

In April 2000, I decided to make money by starting a business buying houses, gutting them, and then rebuilding the interiors to increase their market value. I was good at the job but it was not a good lifestyle for me. Except for the days where I had custody of Ryan, I could keep whatever hours I wanted. I still had problems sleeping at night, so sometimes I would work all night and sleep during the day. Sometimes I worked all night and all the next day. I would often just live on the job site—it was better than going home and facing my empty apartment and trying to sleep. I soon began to work all day and then party at night, sometimes all night. When I didn't sleep at night, I needed energy to get through the next day. That's when I started using coke again. Coke gave me energy to get through the days and nights. It made me feel good about everything for a little while, and when the buzz wore off, there was always more coke. Once that cycle started, I began to completely lose control of my life.

I bought a large ranch house and forty acres of land overlooking the Rocky Mountains. The house was about 20 minutes outside of Calgary and had been divided into little rooms with small windows. I decided to completely gut the interior and create large airy rooms full of natural night. I moved my few possessions into the house and began the demolition.

It didn't occur to me that moving into a house that I was gutting might not be the best thing for my mental health. I had almost completely stopped looking after my emotions and body by that point. I had no sleep schedule. In fact, most of the time I just didn't bother going to sleep. I also didn't bother to eat very much. My body would recover on the days that Ryan came to stay with me, but every time she went back to Jana's, I seemed to party a little harder. It became very hard to ignore how messed up my life was becoming, but somehow I did. I would break a promise because I was drinking; I'd miss an appointment because I was high; I was late because I was hungover—but still, I couldn't admit that addiction had got the better of me. I was losing all of my boundaries. There were people around who just wanted to party with me, only because I was supplying the booze and drugs. They stole from me and mooched off of me but I just didn't care.

The worst thing about the coke was how it isolated me from the people who cared about me: my family and old friends. At least with the booze I could still make public appearances and socialize, but cocaine made me paranoid. I was always paranoid. I couldn't trust people. I was sure that anyone who got close to me would violate me the way Graham had. I began doing regular rounds through the house, checking all of the windows and under the staircases. Eventually, I called up

Jana and told her that I was incapable of looking after Ryan anymore. Jana wanted me to get help but she knew she couldn't force me.

With Ryan gone, I had no one to be accountable to. My house was torn apart and half rebuilt—no furniture, no furnace in the winter, no food in the fridge. It was like living in a crack house. I was utterly helpless because of my addiction. I didn't leave the house unless it was to get more coke. I would buy an ounce of coke at a time and that was what I lived off: coke and the water from the tap. I couldn't breathe through my nose anymore, and sometimes it felt like I couldn't breathe through my mouth. The fear of somebody driving up to my house and seeing me in that state was unbearable. I once locked myself in a hotel room for eight hours so I could do coke without anyone seeing me. My calves were aching from getting up and looking through the hotel door peephole so often. I was destroying my sinuses, destroying my body, and destroying any hope of finding a healthy way of living. I hadn't had the guts to kill myself like I'd wanted to for the last twenty years but I'd finally found a way of living and a drug that would do it for me. I had nobody. I had pushed away every person who ever tried to help me. I'd had a few coke girlfriends in my life during those years but that was about it for companionship. Through it all, I still wanted someone to come up to the house and help me, but I had already pushed everybody away, and even if they had come, I probably wouldn't have answered the door.

I completely isolated myself inside that giant gutted house. I felt like I had gone there to die. I then went on a coke binge that kept me up for seven days straight. By the third day, I was convinced that there were people hiding inside the house. They were after me. I had to find them. I did patrols all day and night through the house carrying my shotgun. I could never find them but I knew people were hiding, waiting for me to let my guard down long enough to pounce on me when I wasn't looking. Finally, I took my gun and my bag of coke and holed myself up in my furnace room, the only safe room in the house, or so I believed. By that point, a gun didn't offer enough protection from all of my enemies, so I left the furnace room long enough to find another weapon: a sledge-hammer. I wasn't going down without a fight.

I had finally hit rock bottom. The only thing left to do was die. I could see that clearly: I was going to die. I was powerless. I had completely lost control. Once I realized that I had no control over my life, that I had *never* had any control over my life and my addictions, something changed inside me. I made a phone call to a friend from California, who got hold of the NHLPA substance abuse program. When they heard how bad I was, they got me a spot in the treatment centre in California. My friend came to Calgary and drove me down to California. My mind and body were a complete mess, but I felt ready for the treatment in a way I never had before. I knew that I was not going down there to deal with the ghost of Graham James but rather with my own addiction problems. Yes, a lot of those problems stemmed from Graham but that was beside the point this time. I had to quit drugs and alcohol or I was going to die. I was going into treatment to deal with my addictions.

From day one, I focused on my total helplessness in the face of my addiction. I had been exposed to the Alcoholics Anonymous (AA) program at the centre before but I had never taken it seriously. I'd told myself that I was too smart for AA. I wasn't an addict, I was just a guy with abuse issues who needed time to heal. I promised myself that I wouldn't fall into that trap this time. It's amazing how much evidence there had been for the last decade or so pointing to the fact that I was an alcoholic, but I was always able to convince myself that I didn't have a drinking or drug problem. That is why the first step in the AA program—admitting that you have no control over your drinking—is so important. By confessing that you have a problem, you finally begin to strip off the masks that every alcoholic wears to protect themselves from facing the truth. Addicts are the world's greatest experts at tricking themselves about their habits. They always have an excuse for their drinking, always a perfectly rational reason for getting high.

Only when you admit that your addiction is the real problem can you start to look it square in the face. I had to stop making excuses. I was an addict, plain and simple, and being an addict meant that I had no power over my behaviour. It was true that I had been badly hurt by some people in my life, especially Graham, but I had gotten that off my chest and started to deal with my feelings. I knew what I had to do to get on with my life and my healing. I had dealt with my problems for twenty years by drinking alcohol and getting high. When I felt bad, I drank, and I felt bad most of the time. Drinking just made me feel worse in the long term, which increased my need to feel better by drinking. The shame and guilt of alcoholism fed the shame and guilt of abuse which fed the shame of alcoholism—on and on it went. I had never learned how to properly respond to life's daily problems because I was constantly battling the legacy of abuse and alcoholism. It's hard to wake up as an adult and realize that you've never learned how to live on a day-to-day basis, but that's what I had to do.

I also had to understand how much my addictions had hurt other people. All alcoholics leave a trail of suffering. My way of making people suffer was through selfishness and through hurting myself. I had been generally nice to people. I even went out of my way not to hurt people but I did hurt them every time I refused to accept help from them. People would try to help me and I would push them away through hostility and clownish behaviour. Now I know that what my friends and family really want is for me take care of myself. Sticking to the AA steps became my way of giving something back to the people who had cared about me for so many years. It became my way of finally stopping the selfishness that ruled my life for so long. I realized that by splitting up with Jana, I was letting her go free to be a woman with her own life. I was not bringing her down anymore and making her suffer my pain. We are now better friends than we ever were. That was one of the smartest, least selfish things I ever did. It made Jana and Ryan's life so much better. I am so grateful for the two of them. If it weren't for them, I could have easily ended up like Martin Kruze or the countless number of sexual abuse victims who have committed suicide.

The AA program works for me, and for millions of other addicts, because it makes certain concepts very simple to understand. The alcoholic needs things simplified for them. This is where the twelve steps come in. They provide a total framework for learning how to live without addiction and the addict learns the steps by talking to people who have gone through the process. The best part is that everyone at an AA meeting is an expert in the psychology of the addict. They know every trick in the alcoholic's book, and they will tell you to your face when they see you try to justify your behaviour with one of those tricks. AA is about so much more than talking about your addiction. Talking to a hardcore alcoholic about their drinking or trying to get them to control their drinking rarely works. I know this from experience. I was in a number of different treatment centres and in every one of them, I managed to convince my counsellor that I was on the road to recovery. I had them convinced that I really wanted to change. But did they really think that a thirty-day or a ninety-day program was going to undo decades of learned behaviour and self-abuse? I had learned to live a certain way for years to protect myself and survive. This behaviour worked in its way, protecting me from the worst of the pain and shame. I wasn't about to let go of those techniques in thirty days. I had no other way of coping with daily life and all of the negative feelings I carried inside me. Learning to live is a process that should start the day you're born, but for me, that process was hijacked at a very early age. AA offered me a way to learn to start living.

I've finally found something in my life that's working. It's not an instant fix but I can see a little more light in my life with every month that passes. AA represents hope to me. It may not work for everybody, but anyone who wants to heal has to find a system that works for them. The AA philosophy and the meetings and the opportunity to meet and help other people with similar problems keeps me going. On one level, the meetings serve the same function that alcohol once did. They make me feel better about myself for a little while. They offer me a place to go to where no one will judge me, a place where everyone understands what I'm going through. But unlike getting drunk, the meetings fill me with positive emotions and give me strength to go back to my life and deal with both the aftermath of the abuse and the challenges of daily life. The twelve-step program has given me the courage to admit that I am an alcoholic and always will be. I know now that I can't have a drink or touch any drugs. If I do, I will go back to that cycle of shame and dependence. One drink would be enough to start everything all over again. And if I relapse, I will know why: because I fell into the old patterns and stopped going to the meetings and sticking to the program. No excuses.

There are times when I look around and wonder how I made it through those twenty years and survived. I wonder how I functioned on a daily basis. I look at my mantelpiece, where the Gemini Award for the film that was made of my life story sits, and I have to laugh: how did I get up on that stage and accept the trophy? How did a movie about my life even get made? How was I able to help the producers? Looking back further, I ask myself how I managed to play in the NHL for almost a decade. How did I help the Broncos win the Memorial Cup or the Canadian juniors win a gold medal? And how the hell did I skate across Canada? I was such a total mess in my head and in my heart that I am blown away that so many good things happened to me. I don't know how I made it through. I guess I've been blessed with some pretty strong survival skills.

I believe in a higher power. I don't always feel comfortable calling that power God, and I've never

Holding the Gemini Award for the CTV production,
The Sheldon Kennedy Story.

been a regular church-goer, but I do believe in a creator. I have faith that I am being watched over and guided and that if I ask for help, I will receive it. Having faith is everything. You have to want to be in this life, and to do that, you have to have faith that things will be okay in the end if you want them to be. I've participated in a number of sweat lodges and fasts with native friends of mine and I've been very enriched by the experiences. There are spirits all around you when you do a sweat, I have no doubt of that now. A friend of mine is a native medicine man in the North, and I have done work on a number of reserves helping people with their own abuse issues. The native spirituality is all about reconnecting with Mother Earth and honouring the people who have come before you, and this teaching has helped me to heal. There is nothing preachy or judgmental about any of the Native teachings I have come into contact with. These teachings are given freely to anyone who really wants them.

I am still haunted by powerfully negative emotions that I connect to the years of sexual- and self-abuse. Some of those negative feelings will probably always be with me but I've finally learned that it's what I do with those feelings that counts. I need to always fight those feelings, to tell myself that what they tell me is not true: I am not worthless. I'm not stupid. I can do what I want in life. I can finally open up to people and love them in return. I can trust people. I can accomplish short-term and long-term goals if I just put my mind to it and stay the course. And if I have any setbacks, then I just have to pick myself up and start again. Those voices in my head might never totally go away but I can choose not to listen to them or obey them.

I'm not sure where I'm going but I know where I'm *not* going. I feel like I am finally learning how to live. Everything is different, it's all new. I'm not just telling the same old story about Graham and what he did to me. Now I'm really in the picture. I have, for the first time ever, a feeling of gratitude. My life is hardly a bed of roses but it's the best it's ever been for me. And I say this knowing that I really don't have a plan for the rest of my life. I trust that God has a plan for me and that I will be strong enough to find it.

Index

Taylor, Teddy, 21
Team Canada, 83
Therapist, 121, 169, 194
Therapy, 69-70, 145, 201,
    212, 214
Tisdale, Tim, 85, 131

Toronto, ON, 53, 155-156,
    182, 184, 210
Toronto Blue Jays, 184
Toronto Maple Leafs, 183-
    184
Training camp, 91, 95,
    105, 130, 136
Trapp, James, 52, 54
Treatment centre, 212-214,
    219
Treatment program, 212-
    214, 219, 222
Tryout camps, 24

United Way, 167
USSR, 83

Vancouver, BC, 142, 165,
    208
Vancouver Island, BC,
    169, 193c
Vooys, Chantelle, 171

Waite, Jimmy, 84
Waiver draft, 110
Western Hockey League
    (WHL), 20, 23, 32, 44,
    53-55, 59-62, 65, 70, 84,

88, 91, 109, 113, 153
    draft, 23
Westerm Report magazine,
    190
Westin Hotel, 162
Willick, Cindy, 171
Wilson, Rosemary, 171
Windsor, ON, 106
Winfrey, Oprah, 148
    Oprah Winfrey Show,
    155
Winnipeg, MB, 11-13, 20,
    30-33, 39, 43-44, 53-54,
    65, 102, 108, 110, 188c
Winnipeg Jets, 110
Winnipeg Monarchs, 20
Winnipeg South Blues, 31,
    34c, 53
Winnipeg Warriors, 32, 44
World Junior
    Championship, 83

Yzerman, Steve, 103